Class-Act
Q·U·I·L·T·S

18 Eclectic Quilts by Teachers and Their Students

That Patchwork Place®

Compiled by Ursula Reikes

CREDITS

Editor-in-Chief . . . . Kerry I. Hoffman
Managing Editor . . . . .Judy Petry
Technical Editor . . . . Ursula Reikes
Copy Editor . . . . Tina Cook
Proofreader . . . . .Melissa Riesland
Cover Designer . . . . .Kay Green
Text Designer . . . . .Joanne Lauterjung
Production Assistant . . . . Shean Bemis
Illustrators . . . . Brian Metz
Bruce Stout
Photographer . . . . Brent Kane

Printed in Hong Kong
01 00 99 98 97 96   6 5 4 3 2 1

Library of Congress Cataloging-in-Publication Data
Class-act quilts : 18 eclectic quilts by teachers and their students /
    compiled by Ursula Reikes.
        p.   cm.
    ISBN 1-56477-151-2
    1. Patchwork.   2. Quilting.   3. Patchwork quilts—Design.
I. Reikes, Ursula
TT835.C574 1996
746.46'041—dc20   96-22456
                                                           CIP

MISSION STATEMENT

WE ARE DEDICATED TO PROVIDING QUALITY PRODUCTS AND
SERVICES THAT INSPIRE CREATIVITY.
WE WORK TOGETHER TO ENRICH THE LIVES WE TOUCH.

That Patchwork Place is a financially responsible ESOP company

CONTENTS

INTRODUCTION

Quilters love to take classes. They are eager to learn everything there is to know about quilting, and it seems they never get enough. Classes are offered at quilt shops, guild retreats, seminars, and conferences around the world. Many quilters travel thousands of miles to learn a new technique or take a class from a particular teacher. Though the reasons for taking classes may vary, there is one thing all quilters have in common—a desire to learn and share with others who are equally passionate about quilting.

Just as quilters love to take classes, quilt teachers love to teach. Teachers from the United States, Canada, and New Zealand are featured in this book. As you read the introduction to each quilt, you'll learn a little about the teacher, the inspiration for her quilt, and why she loves to teach. As with all quilters, teachers also have something in common–they relish the opportunity to share their knowledge and inspire quilters to be creative.

The call for *Class-Act Quilts* was announced in our Top Teachers Club newsletter in the summer of 1995. In addition, we welcomed entries from teachers all over the world.

As the staff reviewed the 150 entries, we concentrated on selecting quilts that represented a variety of styles—from traditional to contemporary—and a variety sizes and techniques. We tried to include projects that would appeal to a wide range of skill levels. There are simple quilts, as well as more complex quilts for those looking for a challenge. There is something for everyone in this collection–quick and easy piecing, piecing with templates, foundation paper piecing, and appliqué.

In order to include as many designs as possible, we did not include instructions on basic quiltmaking techniques. These are readily available in many of That Patchwork Place's other books, some of which may already be on your bookshelf.

I hope you enjoy the class projects we have selected. Now sit back, take a moment to peruse the quilts in this book, and get ready to take a class in the comfort of your own sewing room. You could invite some friends and create your own classroom setting! Now class, let's begin.

Ursula Reikes

VICTORIAN HANKIE POCKETS

By Peggy True

Meet the Teacher

*P*eggy True has enjoyed sewing and related arts since childhood. She was fortunate to live near Houston in the 1970s and participated in the quilt revival, which was just beginning at that time. Grounded in traditional quilting, she has taken the leap into creating original designs and is especially interested in wearable art.

When talking about her teaching, she says, "I love the free exchange of ideas, how we feed each other's creativity! Teaching is its own reward because of the wonderful people I meet. There is never a dull moment in the company of kindred spirits—or is it fabricaholics?"

Peggy lives in Clayton, California, with her husband, Windell, and daughter, Pamela. She teaches for The Guild of Quilters of Contra Costa County and for ThimbleCreek, a favorite quilt shop.

"Victorian Hankie Pockets" is an original wall quilt that features six Pocket blocks based on favorite Victorian motifs: hearts and fans. Embellishments can be added as desired. This quilt design offers a charming display for those lovely, frilly handkerchiefs you've been collecting all these years. Peggy enjoys this class because it is good vehicle for teaching a variety of techniques.

Diana Roberts is an experienced quiltmaker and needle-arts enthusiast. An active member of her guild, she has served many leadership positions.

TEACHER'S QUILT:
Victorian Hankie Pockets *by Peggy True, 1995, Clayton, California, 36¼" x 26¼".*

STUDENT'S QUILT:
Victorian Hankie Pockets *by Diana Roberts, 1995, Concord, California, 16½" x 45".*

Finished Quilt Size: 36¼" x 26¼"

MATERIALS: *44"-wide fabric*

1 yd. small-scale print for background, pocket lining in Fan and Heart blocks, and binding
½ yd. light print for Fan and Heart block backgrounds
¼ yd. light green print for inner border and piecing
½ yd. medium-scale floral for outer border and piecing
¼ yd. each of 4 or 5 small- to medium-scale floral prints that coordinate with the background
1 yd. for backing
34" x 44" piece of batting
2 antique or new doilies, about 5" in diameter
6 antique or new fancy-edged handkerchiefs
Assorted embellishments: lace appliqués, trims, edgings, buttons, ribbon roses, charms
8" square plain muslin
8" square paper-backed fusible web
Template plastic
Tracing paper or photocopies of Template C
Optional: Machine-embroidery thread and needle for decorative stitching

CUTTING

Use Templates on pages 11–13

From the small-scale print, cut:

4 strips, each 2½" x 42", for binding
2 squares, each 7½" x 7½", for center squares
6 of Triangle A for side triangles
4 of Triangle B for corner triangles
3 of Template C for fan lining
2 of Template D for heart lining
2 of Template G for heart top lining

From the light print, cut:

6 squares, each 7½" x 7½", for the Fan and Heart block backgrounds

From the light green print, cut:

4 strips, each 1½" x 42", for inner borders

From the medium-scale floral, cut:

4 strips, each 3" x 42", for outer borders

From all fabrics, cut:

4 strips, each 2¼" x 7½", for heart and fan foundation piecing

ASSEMBLING THE BLOCKS

Finished Block sizes: 7" x 7"

Both the scalloped and pointed fans are a bit more difficult than the basic Fan Block. Those with less sewing experience may want to use the basic Fan Block for all three fans.

Basic Fan Block

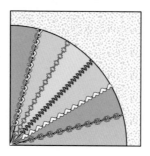

1. Make a photocopy or trace Template C onto tracing paper. Cut out the fan ½" outside the lines. In foundation piecing, fabrics are placed on the unmarked side of the paper foundation and the seams are sewn on the marked side. A light source, such as a lamp or window, is helpful in positioning the fabric.

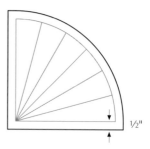

½"

2. From the 2¼" x 7½" strips, select 6 fabrics for the fan blades. Decide on the placement of the strips. Look for good contrast between the blades, and do not use strips from the background fabric for the outer fan blades.

2¼" x 7½" strips

3. Begin by placing the 2 middle fabric strips right sides together. Hold the paper up to the light and position the matched edges of the first 2 strips so a ¼"-wide seam allowance extends past the center sewing line. Pin the fabrics to the unmarked side of the foundation paper.

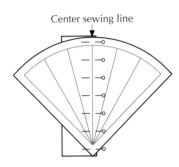

Center sewing line

4. Set your stitch length at 18 to 20 stitches per inch. (The small stitches perforate the paper and make removal easier.) Stitch along the center sewing line, starting at the curve and ending just below the point.

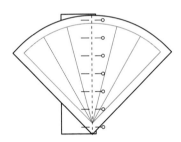

5. Open the strips and press with a dry iron. Continue the piecing toward the sides of the fan, adding a strip at each sewing line. Trim the excess fabric after sewing each seam. Press after adding each piece to keep your work accurate.

6. After all strips have been sewn, trimmed, and pressed, staystitch about ⅛" inside the outer line on the foundation. Trim the fabrics and paper together, cutting on the outer line (which includes a ¼"-wide seam allowance). Do not remove the paper yet.

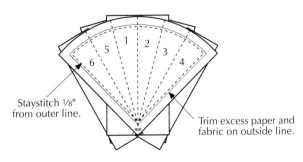

Staystitch ⅛" from outer line.

Trim excess paper and fabric on outside line.

7. Embroider the fan seams as desired, stitching from the top edge toward the point. The paper will serve as a stabilizer. To avoid crowding the decorative stitches at the point, change to a straight stitch for the last ½".

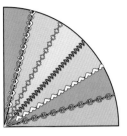

Switch to straight stitch ½" before point.

8. Pin a piece C lining to the fan, right sides together. Sew on the stitching line along the curved edge. Backstitch at both ends to secure the seam. Notch the curved edge.

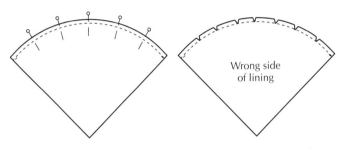

Wrong side of lining

9. Carefully remove the paper. Use tweezers or a seam ripper to remove stubborn pieces. Disregard the small bits caught in the decorative stitching. Turn the fan right side out and press, rolling the lining toward the back side.

10. Pin, then baste the fan to a 7½" light print square, aligning the corner and sides.

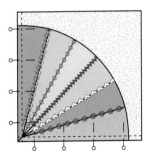

Scalloped Fan Block

Follow steps 1–10 above, except for step 8. Instead, pin a piece C lining to the fan, right sides together, and sew along the stitching line for the scalloped-fan edge. Carefully trim the scalloped seams to ⅛", and clip to the stitching line at the clefts of the scallops.

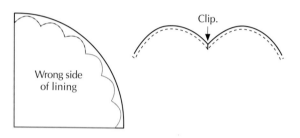

Wrong side of lining

Clip.

Pointed Fan Block

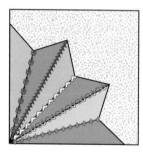

Follow steps 1–10 above, except for step 8. Instead, pin a piece C lining to the fan, right sides together, and sew along the stitching line for the pointed-fan edge. Carefully trim the seams to ⅛", and clip to the stitching line at the clefts of the points. Carefully trim the corners.

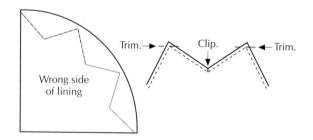

Wrong side of lining

Trim. → Clip. ← Trim.

Easy Appliqué Heart Block

1. Choose any 3 fabrics for layering the hearts. Look for good contrasts, keeping in mind your background fabric. Trace and cut Template D from a selected fabric. Trace Templates E and F onto paper-backed fusible web. Cut out ⅛" outside the drawn line.
2. Fuse the web side of Templates E and F to the wrong side of the selected fabrics, following the manufacturer's instructions. Cut the hearts out exactly on the line, and peel off the paper backing. Stack the hearts as shown and fuse in place. Machine appliqué around the fused edges of the inner hearts using your choice of decorative stitch.

3. Align the piece D lining with the top of the heart, right sides together. Stitch along the top of the heart between the dots, backstitching at each end of the seam. Clip the seam allowance at the dots and in the cleft of the heart. Notch the curves. Turn right side out and press.

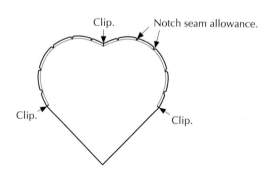

Clip.   Notch seam allowance.

Clip.   Clip.

4. Position the heart on a 7½" light print square, aligning the corner and sides. Pin, then baste inside the ¼"-wide seam allowance. Hand stitch the lower edges of the heart to the square, about 2" on each side.

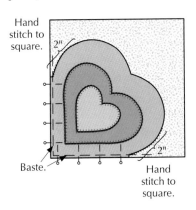

Crazy-Patched Heart Block

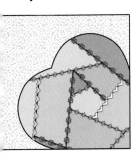

1. Trace and cut Template D from the 8" muslin square. This is the foundation for the crazy piecing. Using the remaining 2¼" x 7½" strips, cover the muslin heart with "sew and flip" patchwork. Begin with a 5-sided center piece placed right side up in the center of the muslin.

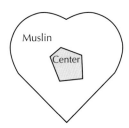

2. Select a strip of fabric for the next piece and place it on the center piece, right sides together. Stitch, using a ¼"-wide seam allowance. Flip the strip open, trim the ends even with the edges of the center piece, and press.

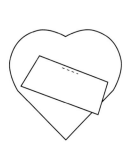
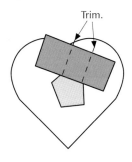

3. Continue adding strips around the center piece, working outward toward the edges. Trim excess seam allowances after adding each piece. When the muslin is covered, trim the patchwork to match the outer edge. If desired, cover the seams with decorative stitches.

4. Repeat steps 3 and 4 of "Easy Appliqué Heart Block."

Woven Heart Block

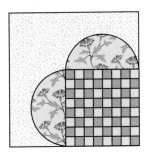

1. Cut 2 of Template G from the selected fabric for the heart tops. Cut 1 strip each, 1½" x 42", from 2 contrasting fabrics that coordinate with the heart tops.
2. Fold the strips in half, wrong sides together, and stitch along the long edge using a ¼"-wide seam allowance. Trim the seam allowance to ⅛". Finger-press the seam open, centering the seam on the back of the tube. Press.

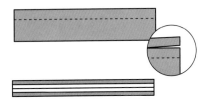

3. Cut 8 segments, each 5" long, from each tube.

4. Place the 8 tube segments from 1 fabric along the straight edge of 1 heart top as shown, right sides together. Join the pieces, using a ¼"-wide seam allowance.

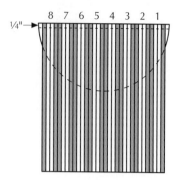

5. Pin, then sew a piece G lining to the heart top along the curved edge. Notch the curved seam allowance and turn right side out.

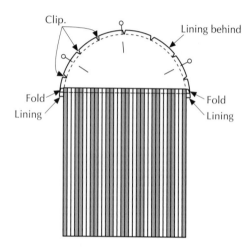

Clip.

Lining behind

Fold Lining

Fold Lining

6. Fold the straight edge of piece G under ¼". Hand stitch the folded edge, covering the ends of the tube and the stitching. Press.

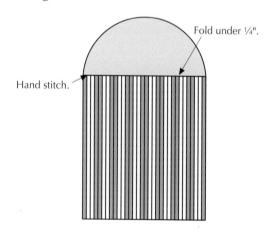

Fold under ¼".

Hand stitch.

7. Repeat steps 4–6 with the contrasting tube segments an second heart top.

8. Position the 2 heart tops as shown on a pinnable surfac such as your ironing board cover. Weave the tubes to gether in a checkerboard pattern. Pull the woven strip together so the surface is snug but not puckered.

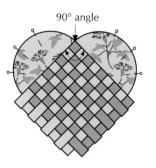

90° angle

9. Pin the heart to a 7½" light print square so the sides of th heart are ¼" from the edge and the tubes extend beyon the edges. Baste the tubes in place, ⅛" from the edge o the square. Trim the tubes even with the edge of th square. Hand stitch the lower edges of the heart tops t the background square as shown, about 2" on each side.

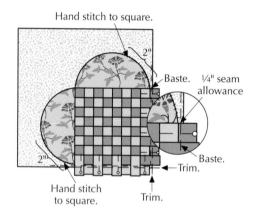

Hand stitch to square.

2"

Baste. ¼" seam allowance

2"

Baste. Trim.

Hand stitch to square.

Trim.

ASSEMBLING THE QUILT TOP & FINISHING

1. Center 1 doily on each 7½" pink minidot square. Hand or machine appliqué in place.
2. Arrange the blocks, side triangles, and corner triangles as shown below. Sew the blocks together in diagonal rows. Press the seams toward the center squares and the side triangles. Join the rows, adding the corner triangles last.

3. Measure the length and width of your quilt to determine the exact length of the borders. Trim the border strips to fit. Add 1½"-wide green inner-border strips to the sides, then to the top and bottom edges of the quilt top. Repeat with the 3"-wide outer border strips.
4. Mark the quilt top with quilting designs of your choice. Peggy quilted a 1" grid in the side and corner triangles.
5. Layer the quilt top with batting and backing; baste.
6. Quilt as desired.
7. Bind the edges and label your quilt. Add a sleeve.
8. Arrange buttons, appliqués, and charms as desired. Hand stitch the embellishments to the hearts and fans. This is where your individuality can really shine! If you love handwork, then show your stuff. Diana's quilt includes handmade ribbon flowers, ruched fabric flowers, silk-ribbon embroidery, and beads.
9. Fold the handkerchiefs off center so all 4 corners can be seen. Try several possibilities. Is there one special corner that deserves to be centered or draped? Look carefully at the photo of "Victorian Hankie Pockets" for ideas.
10. Place the handkerchiefs in the pockets. Hand tack the corners of the handkerchiefs to the quilt. Also tack any drooping spots in the heart and fan pockets.

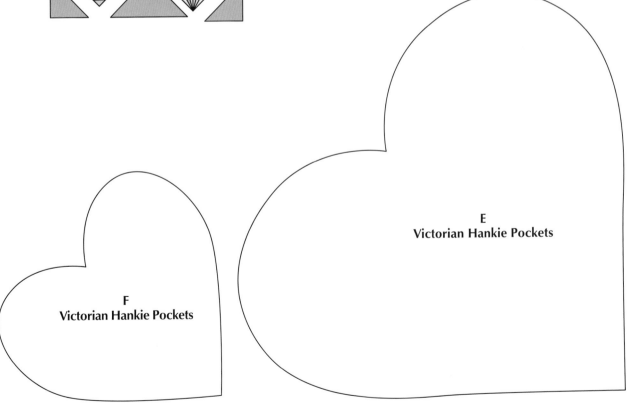

E
Victorian Hankie Pockets

F
Victorian Hankie Pockets

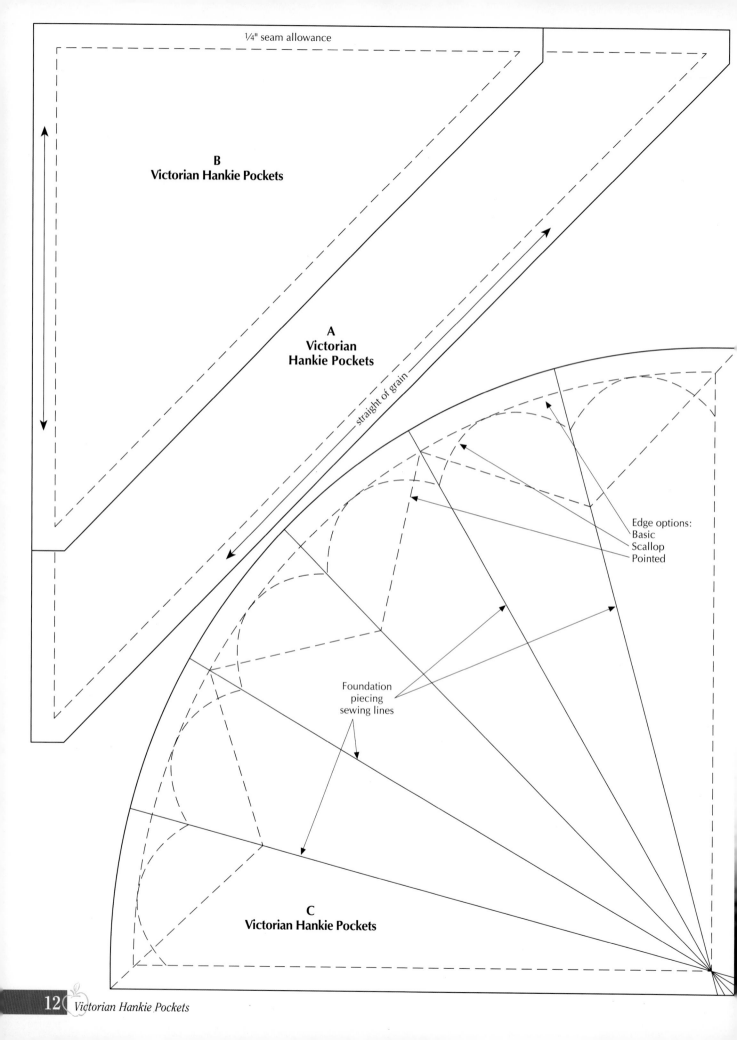

¼" seam allowance

B
Victorian Hankie Pockets

A
Victorian
Hankie Pockets

straight of grain

Edge options:
Basic
Scallop
Pointed

Foundation
piecing
sewing lines

C
Victorian Hankie Pockets

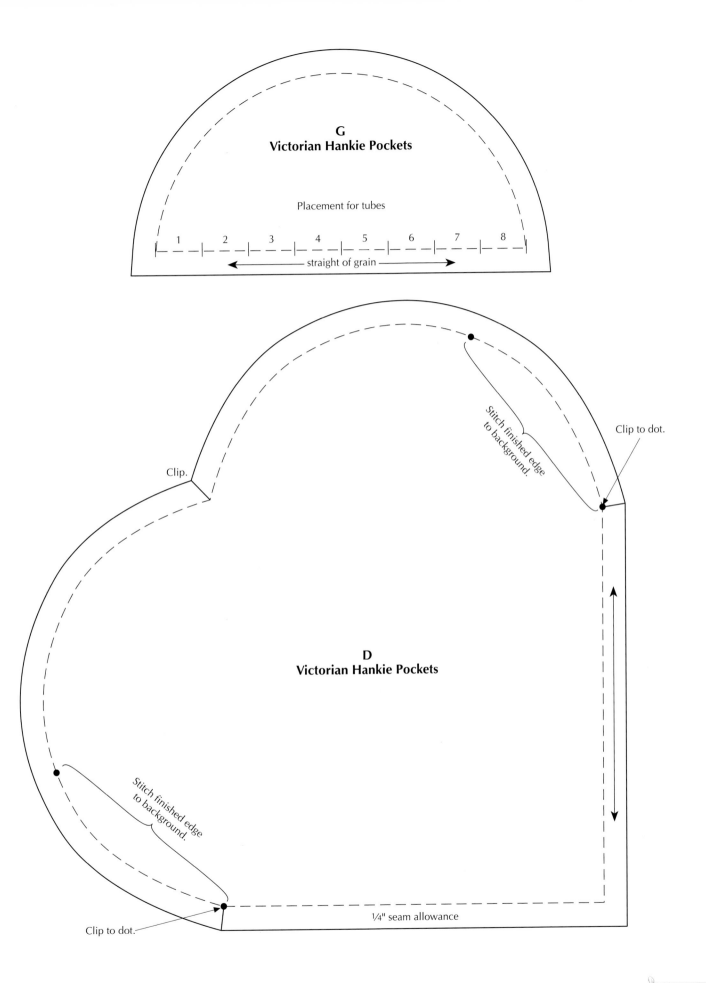

G
Victorian Hankie Pockets

Placement for tubes

1   2   3   4   5   6   7   8

←——— straight of grain ———→

Clip.

Stitch finished edge
to background.

Clip to dot.

D
Victorian Hankie Pockets

Stitch finished edge
to background.

Clip to dot.

1/4" seam allowance

MOSTLY MALTESE

By Joanne Butler Myers

Ardith & Joanne

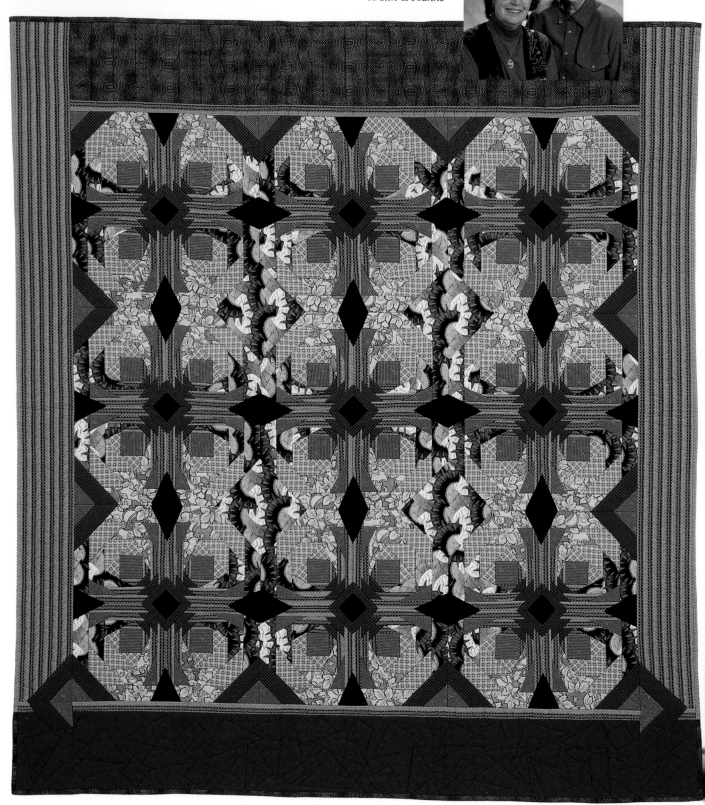

TEACHER'S QUILT: Mostly Maltese *by Joanne Butler Myers, 1994, Bend, Oregon, 65" x 73".*

Meet the Teacher

$\mathcal{J}$oanne Butler Myers's roots are in Tippecanoe County, Indiana, where she inherited a treasured collection of family quilts. After retiring as a dietitian, she joined a quilt guild and discovered why so many women are attracted to quilting—the special bond with other women, which for Joanne includes her own daughters.

The idea of foundation piecing began as a "what if" idea with a friend, Betty Hillenbrand, in Illinois. While Joanne and Betty were admiring an antique New York Beauty quilt, they decided there had to be an easier way to make the complicated pattern other than cutting all those triangles. Their solution was paper piecing.

After Joanne and her husband retired to Oregon, she began teaching paper foundation piecing at the Sisters Quilt Show using her original designs.

Joanne enjoys participating in quilt events and has exhibited her work in national shows. Several of her quilts also have been published in books and magazines.

The inspiration for "Mostly Maltese" came from a fabric in P & B's Kitaamba Collection. The large print became her theme fabric. Joanne then selected eight coordinating fabrics.

Ardith "Ardy" Youngers, student and friend, made "Circles in the Sea" with the same 9" off-center Pineapple block. Her arrangement of light and dark values within the block and her border treatment create a distinctly different quilt from "Mostly Maltese."

STUDENT'S QUILT:
Circles in the Sea
by Ardith Youngers, 1994,
Bend, Oregon, 48½" x 48½".

Finished Quilt Size: 65" x 73"

Directions are provided for making "Mostly Maltese." This design uses two variations of the same block (Blocks A and B) made with the same fabrics in different positions. There are two additional block variations: Blocks AW and BW. They are constructed the same as Blocks A and B through patch 24; however, patches 25 and 26 are eliminated.

If you prefer to make a smaller quilt like Artie's, simply make 16 identical blocks and arrange them in a pleasing design. You will not need to purchase as much fabric for a small quilt.

MATERIALS: 44"-wide fabric

Select a variety of fabrics with strong contrasts in value.

1¼ yds. dark red #1
1¼ yds. light beige
1¼ yds. theme print
1¼ yds. dark red #2
1¼ yds. medium green
⅞ yd. black
4 yds. striped fabric to coordinate with theme fabric and for side borders*
2 yds. dark red #3 for bottom border
2 yds. dark neutral-and-black for top border
4½ yds. for backing (pieced lengthwise)
70" x 76" piece of thin batting

*Joanne's striped fabric had a 2" repeat; a wider repeat will require more fabric.

CUTTING

STRIPS

Fabric	No. of Strips to Cut	Strip Width	Second Cut	Patch No.
Dark red #1	11	2¼"		13, 14, 26
	3	3"	36 squares, each 3" x 3"	
Light beige	15	2¼"		6, 12, 20 (Block A)
				5, 11, 19 (Block B)
Theme print	15	2¼"		5, 11, 19 (Block A)
				6, 12, 20 (Block B)
	1	6¾"	4 squares, each 6¾" x 6¾"	
Dark red #2	18	2¼"		7, 16, 23, 25
Medium green	15	2¼"		3, 4, 8, 15
Black	12	2¼"		21, 22, 24
Stripe*	8	1½"		1, 2, 9, 10, 17, 18

*Cut strips from the entire length of the fabric (lengthwise grain).

TEMPLATES

Fabric	Template	No. of Templates to Cut
Dark red #1	26	4
Dark red #2	25	4

BORDERS

Fabric	No. of Strips to Cut	Strip Width	Borders
Stripe*	2	6"	Side borders
	2	1½"	Top and bottom inner border
Dark neutral-and-black*	1	9"	Top outer border
Dark red #3*	1	9"	Bottom outer border

*Cut strips from the entire length of the fabric (lengthwise grain).

ASSEMBLING THE BLOCKS

Finished Block Size: 9" x 9"

Trace 36 off-center pineapple patterns (on the pullout pattern) onto newsprint, lightweight typing paper, or vellum. Trace all lines and numbers carefully. The numbers indicate fabric placement and piecing order.

Cut out the 9½" x 9½" paper patterns on the outside lines. Note that the ¼"-wide seam allowance is included on the pattern. To piece the blocks, strips of fabric are placed underneath the paper (on the unmarked side), beginning in the center, and sewn in numerical order toward the edges. Stitching is done on the marked side of the pattern, directly on the lines so you can see where you are going.

> *Before starting, I recommend making a test block. This will give you a chance to judge the color and value placement within the block. Cut a 2¼"-wide strip from each fabric and follow the directions in "Assembling the Blocks" to make one block.*
>
> *To preview the block, use two 9" mirror tiles (from a hardware store or glass and mirror shop) taped together at a 90° angle with duct tape. If the edges of your mirror tiles are sharp, cover them with duct tape too. Stand the mirrors on the table in an L shape. Place the completed block between the two mirrors. The reflection will create the illusion of four quilt blocks. At this point, ask yourself, "Do I like what I have sewn?" Quite often, students decide to change the fabric placement within the block to strengthen the design.*

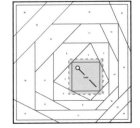

To avoid confusion when placing fabrics, make all the A blocks, then make all the B blocks.

1. Place a 3" dark red #1 square, right side up, on the unmarked side of the paper over the square marked "Center." Hold the paper and fabric up to the light to ensure that the fabric completely covers the Center square, plus at least ¼" beyond the Center on all four sides to provide adequate seam allowance. Pin the fabric in place. Place pins on the printed side of the paper pattern. Check placement again after pinning to make sure the fabric has not shifted.

2. With right sides together, position the 1½" strip of striped fabric on the Center square of fabric so that when sewn and opened up the striped fabric will cover patch 1. The edges of the two fabrics should extend at least ¼" beyond the seam line on the paper pattern. Check the placement by holding the pattern and fabric up to the light. Pin the fabrics in place.

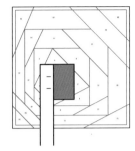

3. Set your sewing machine at 15 to 20 stitches per inch. The small stitch length makes removing the paper much easier. Position the paper, with fabric underneath, under the presser foot so you will be able to stitch on the vertical line between the Center square and patch 1. Stitch on the marked line. Cut the threads and turn the paper over to see the fabric underneath. Trim the seam allowance to ¼". Flip the fabric strip open. Trim the strip just beyond each end of the stitching line. Finger-press the seam open, then press with a dry iron. Do not use steam—it will curl the paper.

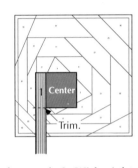

4. Use the same striped fabric strip for patch 2. With right sides together, position the strip at a right angle to the fabric in patch 1. Extend the fabric strip at least ¼" beyond the seam line. Check the placement by holding it up to the light; pin in place. Stitch on the line between the Center and patch 2. Cut the threads and turn the paper over. Trim the seam allowance to ¼". Flip the fabric open. Trim the strip just beyond the end of the stitching line. Finger-press the seam open, then press with a dry iron.

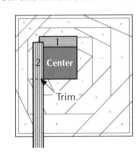

Tip As you add strips, watch for small tucks of fabric at the corners of the points. Use your seam ripper to release the problem fabric and re-stitch the seam if necessary.

5. Repeat the stitch, flip, press, and trim procedure around the center square, adding patches in numerical order. Refer to the block cutting chart to make sure you are using the correct fabric in the correct patch. Remember to position the strip by holding the fabric and paper up to the light before pinning in place.

Make 10 Block A and 8 Block AW (A without patches 25 and 26). Make 10 Block B and 8 Block BW (B without patches 25 and 26).

Block A
Make 10.

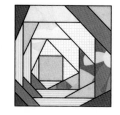

Block B
Make 10.

Block AW
Make 8.

Block BW
Make 8.

6. When the block is complete, trim the fabric even with the edges of the paper. For Blocks AW and BW, trim the diagonal edge ¼" from the line across patches 19, 15, and 20. Do not remove the paper until all the blocks are done.

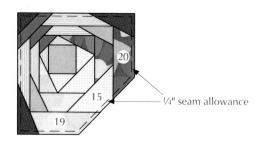

¼" seam allowance

Assembling the Quilt Top

1. Remove the paper from the AW and BW blocks. Use a straight pin to remove tiny pieces. Mark a dot at the ¼" seam intersection on the AW and BW blocks as shown. Mark the ¼" intersections on each corner of the 6¾" theme print square.

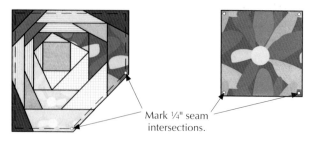

Mark ¼" seam intersections.

2. Sew 2 Blocks AW and 2 Blocks BW together as shown below. Stitch each seam from the outside edge to the dot. Backstitch at the dots.

Start here.

Stop at dot and backstitch.

Make 4.

3. Insert the 6¾" square into the AW/BW unit, matching the dots on the square to the dots on the unit. Pin in place and sew all four sides of the square in a continuous seam. Pivot the block at each dot to continue the seam. To pivot, leave the needle in the down position at the dot, lift the presser foot, and gently turn the fabric to sew the next side. Repeat with each AW/BW unit.

4. Remove the paper from Blocks A and B. Trim any seams to ¼" as needed to tidy up the back.

5. Arrange Blocks A and B around the 4 AW/BW units, rotating blocks as shown below. Sew the 4 AW/BW units together to make the center section. Join the 6 blocks across the top. Join the 4 blocks on each side of the center section. Join the 6 blocks across the bottom. Sew the sections together.

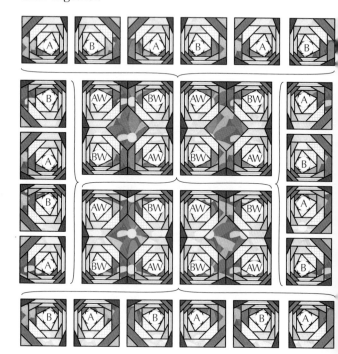

ADDING THE BORDERS

1. Sew an inner border strip to the top outer border on the long edges; treat the resulting unit as a single border strip. Measure the width of the quilt across the center; trim the border strip to that length and sew it to the top of the quilt.
2. Measure the length of the quilt top across the center, including the top border. Trim the side borders to that length. Sew a border strip to both sides of the quilt.
3. Sew the remaining inner-border strip to the bottom outer border along the long edges. Measure the width of the quilt across the center, including the side borders. Trim the border strip to that length and sew it to the bottom of the quilt.
4. Sew pieces 25 and 26 together as shown. Join 2 small pieced triangles to make a large pieced triangle.

5. Turn under a ¼"-wide seam allowance on all edges of the large pieced triangle. Appliqué to the bottom left and right borders, matching the seam lines in the pieced triangle to the seam lines in the adjacent Pineapple block. Align the point of the triangle with the seam line between the side and bottom borders.

FINISHING

1. Layer the quilt top with batting and backing; baste.
2. Quilt as desired. Joanne suggests machine quilting due to the large number of seams in the pieced blocks. She randomly quilted geometric shapes in the borders.
3. Bind the edges of the quilt with leftover strips pieced together.
4. Label your quilt.

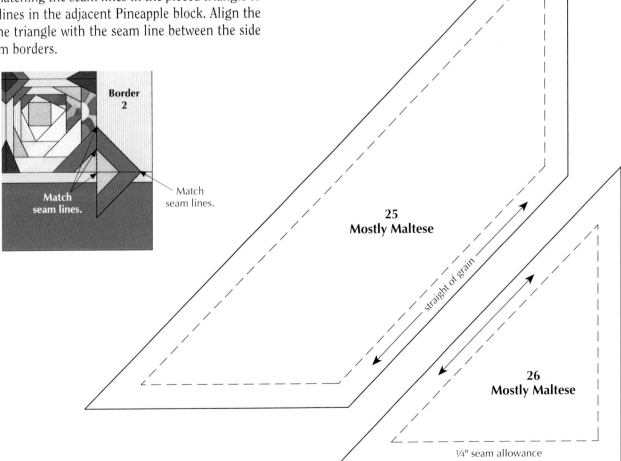

25
Mostly Maltese

straight of grain

26
Mostly Maltese

¼" seam allowance

TEACHER'S QUILT: Rose Red *by Sheila Wintle, 1993, Richmond, Quebec, Canada, 60" x 60".*

Meet the Teacher

$\mathcal{S}$heila Wintle learned to quilt during the quilting revival of 1976. Living in an area devoid of quilting supplies, she found it difficult at first. After completing her first quilt, however, she knew there would be many more to follow. Sheila began teaching adult-education classes and discovered she had a talent for teaching and loved sharing her quiltmaking skills with others.

Quiltmaking has opened the doors to the world of color and design, as well as given Sheila the opportunity to teach many interesting quilters. She encourages her students to follow their instincts. She tells them, "You are here to learn, and my purpose is not to turn out a clone of me, but to empower you to do your own thing."

Sheila lives with her parents and other family members on the family dairy farm in the Eastern Townships of Quebec. Sheila and her mother started their own custom-quiltmaking business, and they enjoy quilting together every day.

"Rose Red" is Sheila's favorite style of quilt— appliquéd and pieced. It was her entry in the Canadian National Quilt Show in 1993, and she received an Honorable Mention. Sheila likes to teach this particular class because it features precise piecing as well intricate appliqué.

Sandi Pope, owner of The Quilters Helper in Ottawa, Ontario, participated in the class with her customers. She is a busy lady and only had time to create the center. Her border design is an adaptation of the ribbon tails with a single rose.

STUDENT'S QUILT: Pink Roses and Purple Ribbons *by Sandi Pope, 1995, Ottowa, Ontario, Canada, 58½" x 58½".*

Finished Quilt Size: 60" x 60"

MATERIALS: *44"-wide fabric*

3 yds. black large-scale floral for piecing, border, and binding
2½ yds. for background
½ yd. *each* of 8 red prints, ranging from light to dark, for roses and piecing
¾ yd. medium green print for leaves and piecing
¾ yd. light yellow print for appliqué and optional piping
½ yd. light gold print for appliqué
½ yd. *each* of light and dark green prints for leaves and piecing
3⅔ yds. for backing (pieced lengthwise)
65" x 65" piece of batting
Template plastic
Fine-point marking pencil
#10 milliners needles for appliqué
#60 Mettler cotton thread to match appliqué fabrics

CUTTING

Make plastic templates of Templates A–J on pages 25–27. Trace around the shapes with a fine-point marking pencil. Cut the pieces on the drawn line.

From the black floral, cut:

4 strips from the lengthwise grain, each 2½" x 64"
4 of Template D

From the background fabric, cut:

1 circle, 18½" in diameter
2 squares, each 21⅜" x 21⅜"; cut the squares once diagonally to yield 4 half-square triangles

Compass

Fabric	Template	No. to Cut
Black floral	A	16
Asst. red prints	B	8
Medium green print	B	8
Background	C	32

Inner Pieced Border

Fabric	Template	No. to Cut
Asst. red prints	E	68
Medium green print	F	64
	H	4 & 4 reversed
Background	G	64
	I	4 & 4 reversed

Outer Pieced Border

Fabric	Template	No. to Cut
Asst. red prints	E	88
Medium green print	F	80
	H	4 & 4 reversed
Background	G	80
	I	4 & 4 reversed
	J	4 & 4 reversed

ASSEMBLING THE COMPASS RING

The templates have clipped corners for easier piecing. Align templates as shown and use a ¼"-wide seam allowance.

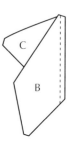

1. Sew 2 background piece C to a red piece B. Sew 2 background piece C to a green piece B. Press the seams toward piece B. Make 8 red and 8 green pieced wedges.

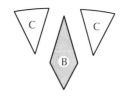

Make 8 red.   Make 8 green.

Check to be sure there is a ¼"-wide seam allowance at the top of the wedge.

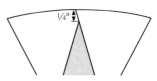

2. To make the compass circle, sew black floral piece A between the pieced wedges, alternating the red and green.

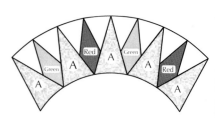

3. Fold the 18½"-diameter circle and compass ring in quarters and lightly press the folds.

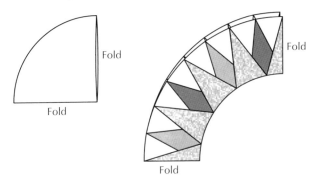

Fold
Fold
Fold
Fold

4. Unfold the circle and compass ring. Match and pin the creases on the circle to the creases on the compass ring. Continue pinning around the circle, easing in fullness, if necessary, as you pin. Sew the pieces together with a ¼"-wide seam allowance. If there is a piece with extra fullness, place it at the bottom.

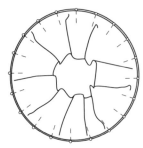

5. To make the set-in square, sew the 4 black floral piece D together as shown.

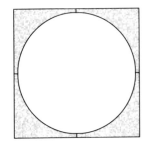

6. If you wish to add flat-edge piping between the compass and the set-in square, see "Flat-Edge Piping" above right.
7. Match and pin the creases on the compass ring with the seams of the set-in square. Continue pinning around the circle, easing in fullness if necessary as you pin. Sew the pieces together with a ¼"-wide seam allowance. If there is a piece with extra fullness, place it at the bottom.

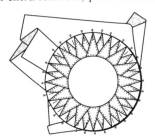

Flat-Edge Piping

If your points are less than perfect, this is a clever way to hide them. Cut ¾"-wide bias strips and join them with a diagonal seam to make one continuous strip approximately 96" long. Fold the strip in half lengthwise and press. Match the raw edges of the piping with the raw edges of the compass circle and pin the piping in place. Carefully ease the piping around the circle so it will lie flat. Baste in place. Continue with step 7 below left.

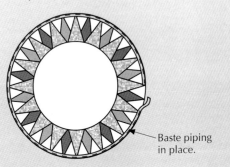

Baste piping in place.

Pieced Inner Border

1. Sew a red piece E to a green piece F.

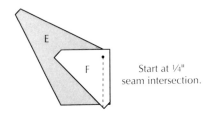

E

F

Start at ¼" seam intersection.

2. Sew a background piece G to piece E/F.

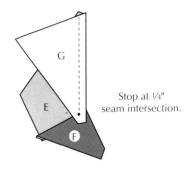

G

E

F

Stop at ¼" seam intersection.

3. Add another red piece E to piece E/F/G in 2 steps. Sew the long side first, stopping at the ¼" seam intersection. Leave the needle down. Pivot piece E to sew the second seam; stitch. Press the seams toward piece E.

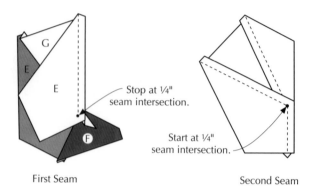

First Seam   Second Seam

4. Continue sewing pieces E, F, and G together to make 4 inner pieced borders. Add pieces H and H reversed and I and I reversed to the ends as shown.

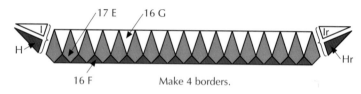

Make 4 borders.

5. Sew the inner pieced border strips to the sides of the quilt, stopping and starting the stitching ¼" from the ends. Miter the corners.

$\mathcal{P}$IECED MIDDLE BORDER

1. Join pieces E, F, and G as described for the inner pieced border above. Make 8 left borders and 8 right borders, adding pieces H, I, and J and H, I, and J reversed as shown.

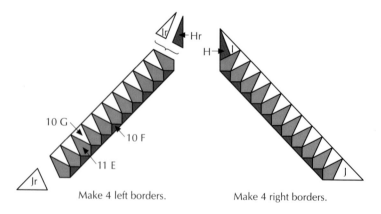

Make 4 left borders.   Make 4 right borders.

2. To prevent stretching, staystitch along the long bias edges of the background half-square triangles. Sew left and right middle pieced borders to the short sides of the triangles. Start stitching at the base of the triangle, then stop ¼" from the top of the triangle. Miter the corners.

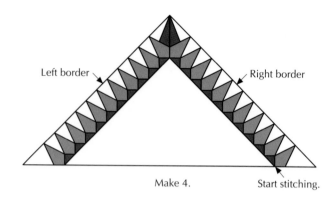

Make 4.   Start stitching.

3. Sew the pieced triangles to the sides of the quilt.

$\mathcal{O}$UTER BORDER

Add the 2½"-wide black floral strips to the sides of the quilt and miter the corners.

$\mathcal{A}$PPLIQUÉING THE ROSES & RIBBONS

Use the Appliqué Placement Guide on the pullout pattern.
1. With the help of a light box or window, use a marking pencil to lightly trace the appliqué design on the inner circle and the half-square triangles.
2. Trace the appliqué shapes on the right side of the appliqué fabric with a fine-point marking pencil. The pencil line will be your turn-under line for needle-turn appliqué. Cut appliqué pieces from the appropriate fabric, adding ¼"-wide seam allowances all around.

3. To appliqué the inner circle, start with the ribbon tails, then add the stems. To make stems, cut bias strips ¾" wide and fold lengthwise in thirds. Spray with starch and press to keep the edges folded.

Appliqué the leaves, roses, and rosebuds, then finish with the bow loops. Clip curves as needed.

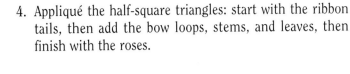

Fold

Fold

Reverse-Appliqué Rosebuds

The center of the rosebud is reverse appliquéd. Before appliquéing piece 6, lightly draw the shape of piece 7 on the right side of piece 6. Cut a small piece of fabric slightly larger than piece 7 and place it underneath the drawn shape.

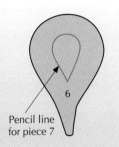

6

Pencil line for piece 7

Appliqué piece 6. Within the drawn outline of piece 7, carefully make a slit on the top fabric only. Trim to within ⅛" of the line. Make sure the fabric for piece 7 is showing through. Turn the cut edges under and stitch in place.

Fabric for piece 7

6

4. Appliqué the half-square triangles: start with the ribbon tails, then add the bow loops, stems, and leaves, then finish with the roses.

FINISHING

1. Layer the quilt top with batting and backing; baste.
2. Quilt as desired. Use the plume quilting design on the pullout pattern for the half-square triangles. Outline-quilt the compass points and pieced borders.
3. To bring the yellow accent color to the outer edges of the quilt, Sheila added a flat-edge piping between the outer border and the binding. Referring to "Flat-Edge Piping" on page 23, cut 1"-wide bias strips and join them to make one continuous piece of piping approximately 244" long. Cut the piping into 4 strips, each 61" long. Matching the raw edges of the piping with the raw edges of the quilt top, pin or baste a length of piping to each edge.
4. Bind the edges and label your quilt.

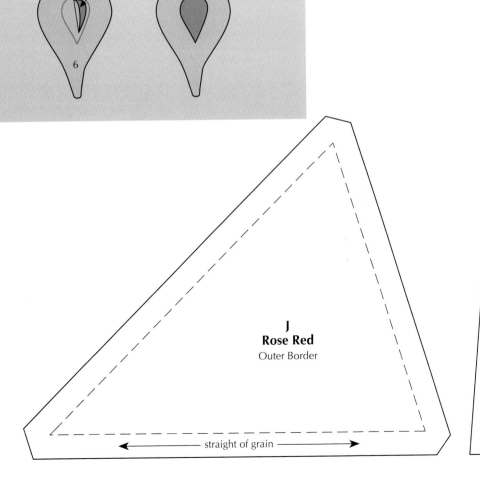

J
Rose Red
Outer Border

straight of grain

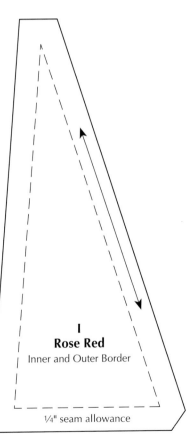

I
Rose Red
Inner and Outer Border

¼" seam allowance

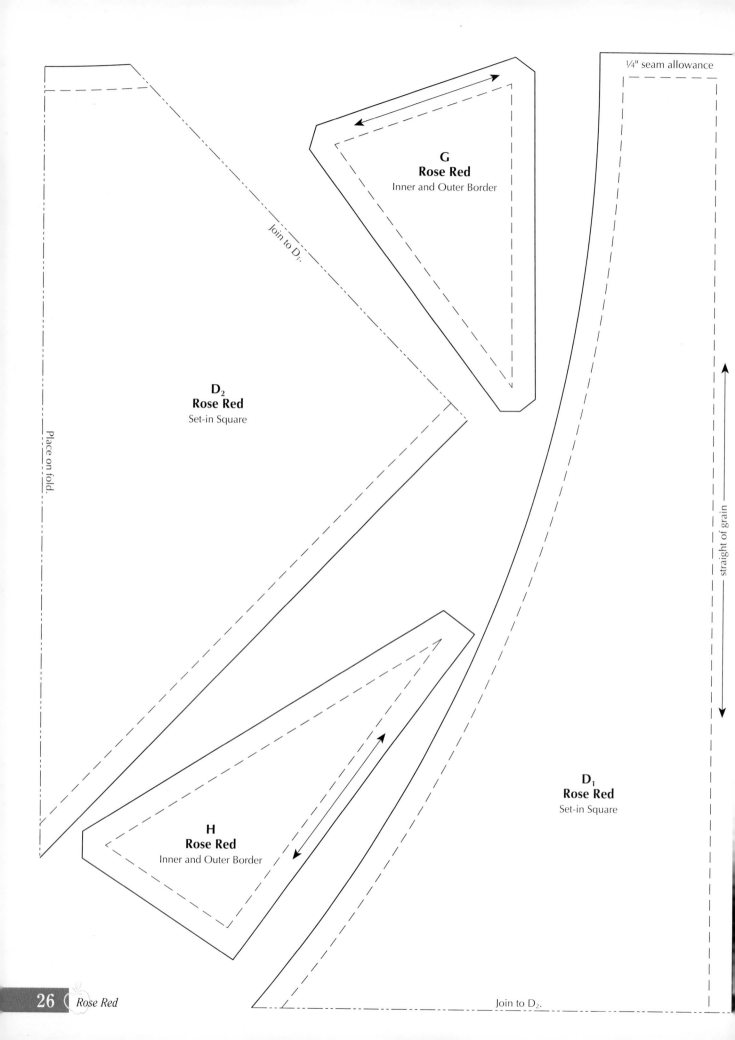

¼" seam allowance

Join to D₁.

G
Rose Red
Inner and Outer Border

D₂
Rose Red
Set-in Square

Place on fold.

straight of grain

D₁
Rose Red
Set-in Square

H
Rose Red
Inner and Outer Border

Join to D₂.

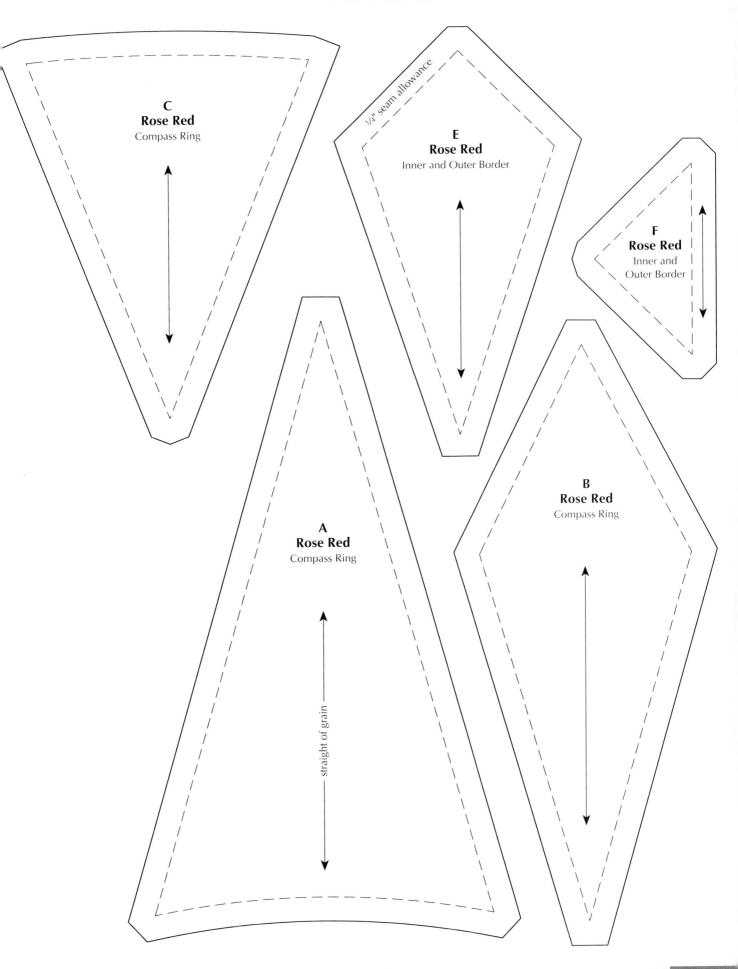

C
Rose Red
Compass Ring

E
Rose Red
Inner and Outer Border

¼" seam allowance

F
Rose Red
Inner and
Outer Border

A
Rose Red
Compass Ring

straight of grain

B
Rose Red
Compass Ring

By Julie Larsen

TEACHER'S QUILT: Crowsfeet *by Julie Larsen, 1995, Kimballton, Iowa, 86" x 111".*

Meet the Teacher

A third-generation quilter, Julie's love of quilting grew from a background in folk art and an interest in collecting antique quilts. In 1986 she started working at a local quilt shop, and soon her earlier career as an English teacher led her to teaching quiltmaking.

Julie believes quilt workshops should be fun as well as educational. She loves teaching in retreat settings because students can interact for more than one day. With her teaching partners Sharlot Steen and Pam Kuehl, Julie founded Iowa's Run-away Quilter's Retreat in 1992. That same year, she purchased the shop where she worked and renamed it "Prairie Star Quilts."

Her love of old quilts leads Julie to create designs with an antique feel. Since her quilts are usually designed with a successful class experience in mind, she likes "Crowsfeet's" large blocks, easy technique, and fast assembly. Julie suggests using a large variety of fabrics in this quilt. It's a great way to put an extensive fat-quarter collection to good use.

Seven of Julie's patterns have been published, and in 1995 she published her first book, Prairie Star Calendar Sampler. Julie makes her home in Kimballton, Iowa, with her husband, Charles.

Student Karma Sorensen of Elk Horn, Iowa, took the Crowsfeet class at Runaway Quilter's Retreat IV. She enlarged the quilt by making the borders wider than called for in the directions.

STUDENT'S QUILT: Crowsfeet *by Karma Sorensen, 1995, Elk Horn, Iowa, 102" x 128".*

Finished Quilt Size: 86" x 111"

MATERIALS: *44"-wide fabric*

¼ yd. each of 18 dark plaids or prints for blocks (or 18 fat quarters, 18" x 22")
⅛ yd. each of 18 light plaids or prints for blocks (or 18 fat eighths, 9" x 22")
⅛ yd. each of 24 light plaids or prints for sashing strips and cornerstones (or 24 fat eighths)
3¼ yds. brown print for side triangles, corner triangles, and middle border
3¼ yds. striped fabric for inner and outer borders
6½ yds. for backing (pieced lengthwise)*
94" x 118" piece of thin batting
1 yd. brown print for 408" of bias binding

If your fabric is less than 44" wide after preshrinking, you will need 7¾ yards for a backing (pieced crosswise).

CUTTING

From each of the 18 dark plaids or prints, cut:

2 squares, each 3½" x 3½"
2 rectangles, each 3½" x 9½"
8 rectangles, each 2" x 3½"
16 squares, each 2" x 2"

From each of the 18 light plaids or prints, cut:

9 squares, each 3½" x 3½"
8 rectangles, each 2" x 3½"

From the 24 light plaids or prints, cut:

2 rectangles from *each* fabric, each 3½" x 15½", for a total of 48 rectangles for sashing strips
A total of 17 squares, each 3½" x 3½", for cornerstones

From the brown print, cut:

4 strips *from the lengthwise grain,* each 3" wide, for middle border
3 squares, each 23" x 23"; cut squares twice diagonally to yield 12 large side triangles (You will use only 10.)
2 squares, each 12" x 12"; cut squares once diagonally to yield 4 corner triangles
4 squares, each 5½" x 5½"; cut squares twice diagonally to yield 16 small side triangles (You will use only 14.)

From the striped fabric, cut:

8 strips, each 1¾" wide (or the width that works best for your stripe), from the length of fabric for the inner and outer borders

ASSEMBLING THE BLOCKS

Finished Block Size: 15" x 15"

For each block, make 8 of the following units. Use only 1 light and 1 dark fabric for each block.

1. Draw a diagonal line on the wrong side of each 2" dark square.

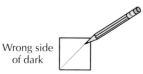

Wrong side of dark

2. With right sides together, place a marked 2" dark square on the left side of a 2" x 3½" light rectangle. Sew on the diagonal line. Trim the seam allowance to ¼" and set aside the cutaway triangles for another project. Press the seam toward the dark triangle. Repeat with a marked 2" dark square on the right side of the rectangle.

Stitch.   Trim.   Press.

Stitch.   Trim.   Press.
                              Make 8 for
                              each block.

3. Sew the pieced unit to a 2" x 3½" dark rectangle.

Make 8 for
each block.

4. Arrange the pieced units, 3½" light squares, 3½" dark squares, and 3½" x 9½" dark rectangles as shown. Join the units in rows, then join the rows to complete a Crowsfeet block. Make 18 blocks.

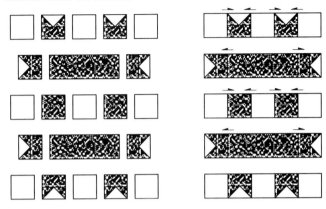

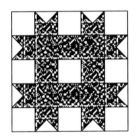

Make 18.

$\mathcal{A}$SSEMBLING THE QUILT TOP & FINISHING

1. Arrange the blocks, sashing strips, cornerstones, side and corner triangles as shown. The side and corner triangles are larger than necessary and will be trimmed after the quilt has been assembled. Sew the blocks and sashing strips together in diagonal rows. Add the large side triangles to the end of each row. Sew the sashing strips and cornerstones in diagonal rows. Add the small side triangles to the end of each row. Press the seams toward the sashing strips. Join the rows. Add the corner triangles last.

2. To trim the oversized side and corner triangles, align the ¼" line on the ruler with the sashing-strip points. Trim the quilt edges ¼" from the bases of the triangles.

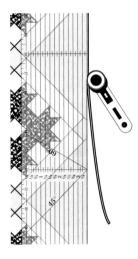

3. Sew a 1¾"-wide striped border strip to each long side of the 3"-wide brown middle-border strips. Press the seams toward the brown strip.

Stripe
Brown
Stripe

4. Sew the borders to the sides of the quilt top and miter the corners. Before stitching the mitered corner, check to make sure the seam lines match perfectly.

5. Layer the quilt top with batting and backing; baste.
6. Quilt as desired.
7. Bind the edges with bias strips and label your quilt.

PAPER DOLL QUILT
By Sue Linker

TEACHER'S QUILT: Paper Doll Baby Quilt *by Sue Linker, 1993, Sumner, Washington, 44½" x 49½".*

Meet the Teacher

*S*ue Linker, author of Sunbonnet Sue All Through the Year, *is a quilting instructor and grandmother of ten. Unfortunately, the grandchildren came along faster than the baby quilts, so she gave up trying to keep pace.*

She is working on a series of baby-quilt designs so each grandchild will have one to present to his or her firstborn. The oldest grandchild is twelve, so Sue hopes to have each special piece by the time it is needed. "Paper Doll Quilt" is one of those.

Sue has no particular quilting or sewing tradition in her background. She was a high-school English teacher before moving twenty years ago to Washington State, where she discovered fabric and quilts. She specializes in hand appliqué and hand quilting and has been teaching throughout the Pacific Northwest for seventeen years.

What Sue likes best about quilting is the quilters. They are special people. Sue views herself as a cheerleader and facilitator, and she encourages students to take her instructions and patterns and do it their own way.

The student quilt was made by Ursula Reikes, a That Patchwork Place editor and good friend. Ursula does wonderful machine appliqué and machine quilting.

This little quilt gives you the choice to do it slowly or do it quickly. Enjoy.

STUDENT'S QUILT: Paper Dolls *by Ursula Reikes, 1995, Redmond, Washington, 44½" x 49½".*

Finished Size: 44½" x 49½"

MATERIALS: *44"-wide fabric*

1⅝ yds. blue-and-white plaid for outer borders and paper doll background

⅓ yd. red print #1 for inner border and 1 sashing strip

⅛ yd. *each* of blue, purple, and green prints for sashing strips

¼ yd. red-and-white stripe for heart background

⅓ yd. red print #2 for hearts

¼ yd. blue-and-white check for bow background

⅓ yd. blue print for bows

¼ yd. yellow-and-purple stripe for butterfly background

⅓ yd. purple print for butterflies

¼ yd. green-and-white check for flower background

⅓ yd. yellow print for flowers

⅓ yd. green print for stems and leaves

½ yd. for bias binding

1½ yds. for backing*

48" x 54" piece of batting

Optional: 1⅜ yds. red print #3 for scalloped cutwork border

This will not be wide enough for the backing. Add leftover fabric from the front of the quilt to make a backing large enough, or buy 2¾ yds. and piece the backing from one fabric.

CUTTING & PIECING STRIPS

Heart Strip

1 strip, 5½" x 33½", from red-and-white stripe
1 strip, 5½" x 33½", from red print #2

Bow Strip

1 strip, 5½" x 33½", from blue-and-white check
1 strip, 5½" x 33½", from blue print

Butterfly Strip

1 strip, 7½" x 33½", from yellow-and-purple stripe
1 strip, 7½" x 33½", from purple print

Flower Strip

1 strip, 6½" x 33½", from green-and-white check
1 strip, 3½" x 33½", from green print
1 strip, 3½" x 33½", from yellow print. Join the green and yellow prints on the long edges, using a ¼"-wide seam

allowance. Press the seam open. *Optional:* For flowers and stems from a single print, cut 1 strip, 6½" x 33½", from desired fabric.

Paper Doll Strip

1 strip, 9½" x 33½", from blue-and-white plaid
1 rectangle, 6¾" x 9½", from *each* of the red, purple, and yellow prints
1 rectangle, 7⅛" x 9½", from *each* of the blue and green prints. Join the rectangles on the 9½" edges, using a ¼"-wide seam allowance. Place the blue and green rectangles at either end. Press the seams open. *Optional:* For paper dolls from a single print, cut 1 strip, 9½" x 33½", from desired fabric.

From each of the blue, purple, and green prints, cut:

1 strip, 2" x 33½", for sashing strips (3 strips total)

From red print #1, cut:

1 strip, 2" x 33½", for sashing strip
2 strips, each 2" x 38½", for inner side borders
2 strips, each 2" x 36½", for inner top and bottom borders

From the lengthwise grain *of the blue-and-white plaid, cut:*

2 strips, each 4½" x 41½", for outer side borders
2 strips, each 4½" x 44½", for outer top and bottom borders

From the lengthwise grain *of red print #3 for the optional cutwork border, cut:*

2 strips, each 3" x 41½", for outer side borders
2 strips, each 3" x 36½", for outer top and bottom borders
4 of Template 7, adding a ¼"-wide seam allowance on curved edge

PREPARING & STITCHING THE PATTERNS

Follow the steps below for hand appliqué; refer to page 36 for machine appliqué:

1. Make cardboard or plastic templates for Templates 1–5 (pages 37–39).
2. Cut freezer-paper strips the same length and width as the background strips for each set of motifs.
3. Fold the strips in half crosswise, shiny side together.
4. Beginning at the center fold of a freezer-paper strip, trace around each template, joining the edges and centering each one between the top and bottom of the strip. For the

paper doll motif, place the center of the motif on the center fold and trace, then trace 2 full motifs. Round off the ends of each motif at each end of the strips.

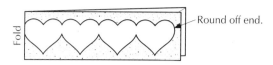

5. With the freezer paper still folded, cut out the string of motifs. Iron together the freezer-paper edges outside the design area to help stabilize the paper as you cut.

6. Place the freezer-paper strip on the right side of the appropriate fabric strips, matching the center fold of the paper strip with the mid-point of the fabric strip. Match the line between the flower and stem pattern to the horizontal seam of the yellow-and-green strip. Place the middle of the paper doll hands on the seams between the colored rectangles. Lightly iron the freezer-paper strips in place.

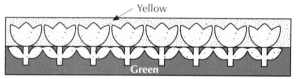

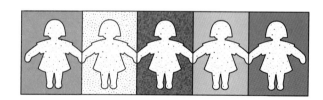

7. Trace the motifs onto the fabric with a pencil or marker you can easily see. Use this line as the guide for needle-turn appliqué. Do not cut out the motifs from the fabric strips. Remove the freezer paper.

8. Baste each motif strip to the same-size background strip. Baste around the outside edges of the strips as well as inside the motifs.

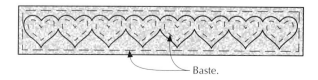
Baste.

9. Beginning at the right end of each strip (or from the left if you are left-handed), cut the motif strip to within ⅛" of the drawn line. Cut away only a few inches at a time. Be careful not to snip the background fabric. Match your thread to each of the appliqué motifs and needle-turn appliqué the motifs in place. Clip where necessary on inside curves and at clefts.

ASSEMBLING THE QUILT & ADDING BORDERS

Directions are provided for making straight-cut borders and the cutwork border shown on page 32.

Straight-Cut Border

1. Sew the 2" x 33½" sashing strips between the rows of motifs. Refer to the photo on page 32.
2. Add the inner borders to the sides first, then to the top and bottom edges.
3. If you wish to add the optional cutwork border, see below. Otherwise, add the outer borders to the sides first, then to the top and bottom edges, then skip to "Finishing" on page 32.

Optional Cutwork Border

1. From freezer paper, cut:
   1 strip, 2½" x 42½"
   1 strip, 2½" x 44½"
2. Fold the paper strips in half, shiny side together.

Fold

3. Make a template of the border scallops on pages 37–38.
4. On one-half of the folded pieces, position the midpoint of the scallop on the fold; trace along the top of the half scallop. Move the template to the left, next to the scallop you just traced, and trace along the top again. Trace a total of 5½ scallops for the side borders, and 4½ scallops for the top and bottom borders. Add ¼" to the end of the last scallop for seam allowances.

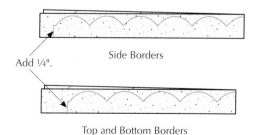
Add ¼".   Side Borders

Top and Bottom Borders

5. Cut the designs from the freezer-paper strips.

6. Beginning with a side border, align the straight edge of the freezer-paper pattern with the long, straight edge of a red print #3 border strip. Match the center of the pattern to the center of the border strip.

7. Lightly iron the freezer-paper border pattern to the fabric.

8. Using a pencil or other marking tool, draw a line right next to the freezer paper. This is the turn-under line. Remove the freezer-paper pattern and reuse it on the next border piece.

9. Lay the 3"-wide red border strip on top of the 4½"-wide background border strip. Match the 2 long, straight edges.

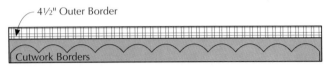

Side Borders

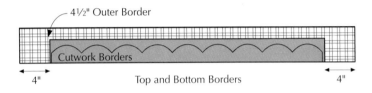

Top and Bottom Borders

NOTE: On the top and bottom background border strips, you should have 4" of fabric at each end for the corner scallops. These will be appliquéd last.

10. Baste the border strips together, ½" from the inside of the drawn line and ½" from the straight edge.

11. Beginning at one end, cut ⅛" from the drawn line and needle-turn the edge. Cut ahead of your stitching, about 5" or 6" at a time. Do not appliqué the ends of the scallops; they will be covered by the corner scallops.

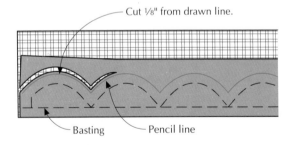

12. Repeat steps 6–11 for the remaining borders.

13. Sew the side borders to the quilt first, then add the top and bottom borders.

14. Turn under the curved edges of the corner scallops (Template 7) and appliqué 1 in each corner.

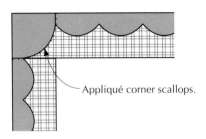

Appliqué corner scallops.

15. To give the quilt a rounded corner, draw around a saucer, jar, lid, or whatever gives you the curve you wish. Trim the corner.

Finishing

1. Layer the quilt with batting and backing; baste.

2. Quilt as desired. Try using #8 perle cotton for outlining the motifs. It adds a nice design element to the quilt. Remember, when using heavier thread for quilting, take larger stitches and try to keep them even.

3. Bind the edges, making sure to use bias strips if your quilt has curved edges. Label your quilt.

To machine appliqué the motifs:

1. Trace the motifs onto a paper-backed fusible web instead of freezer paper (see steps 1–4, page 34).

2. With the strip still folded in half, cut out the string of motifs.

3. Following the manufacturers directions, iron the strip of paper-backed fusible web onto the wrong side of the appropriate print strip.

4. Cut the strip of appliqué motifs from the fabric. Do not cut between the motifs.

5. Fold each background strip in half and crease the center. Position the appliqué motifs on the background strip, centering each one evenly. Be careful not to stretch the appliqué strip while placing it on the background strip.

6. Press the appliqué motifs in place.

7. Machine appliqué the raw edges of the motifs, using a tear-away stabilizer under the fabric.

8. Assemble and finish the quilt as directed above.

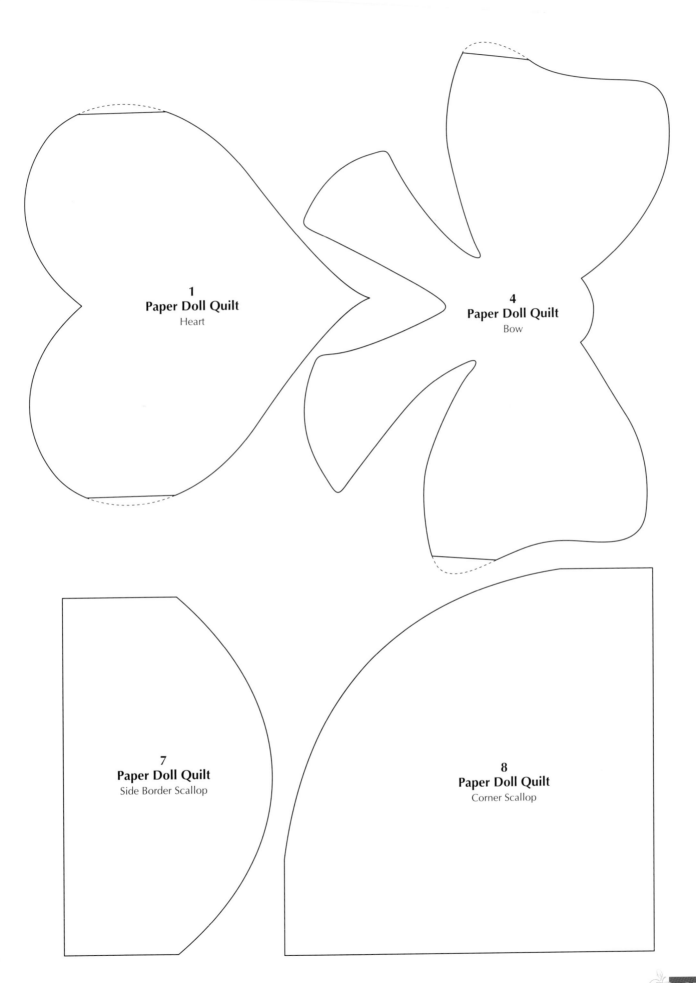

1
Paper Doll Quilt
Heart

4
Paper Doll Quilt
Bow

7
Paper Doll Quilt
Side Border Scallop

8
Paper Doll Quilt
Corner Scallop

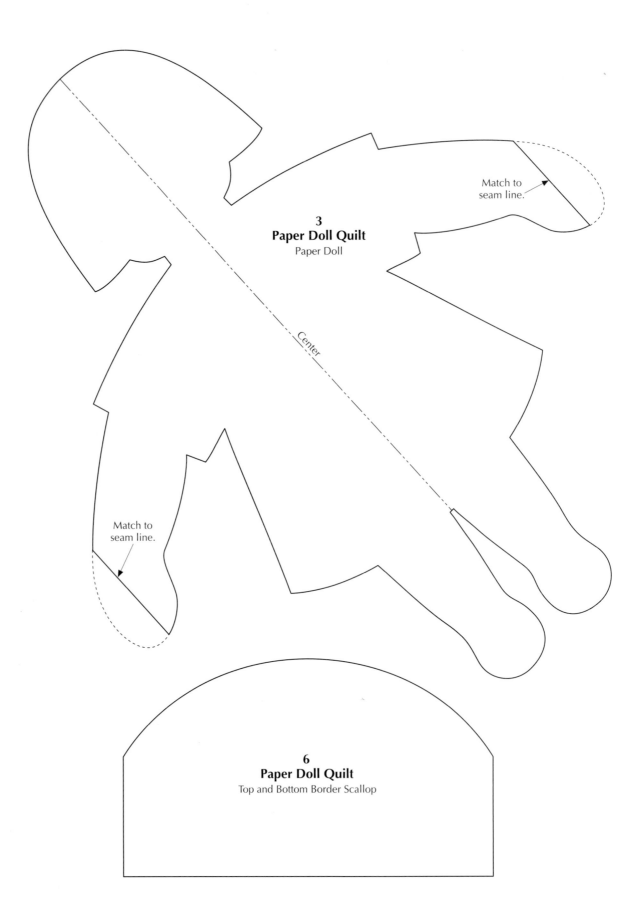

Match to
seam line.

3
Paper Doll Quilt
Paper Doll

Center

Match to
seam line.

6
Paper Doll Quilt
Top and Bottom Border Scallop

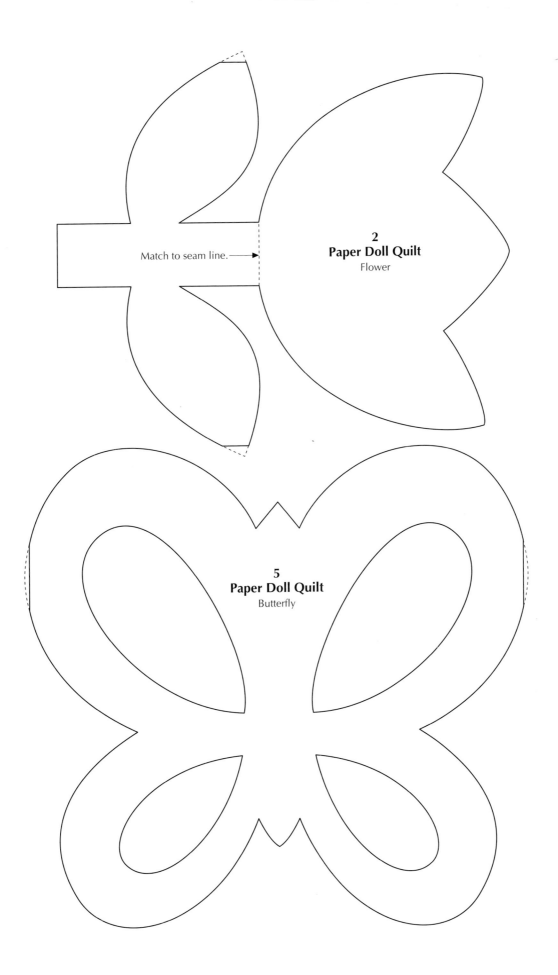

Match to seam line. →

2
Paper Doll Quilt
Flower

5
Paper Doll Quilt
Butterfly

TEACHER'S QUILT: The Wave *by Connie Stillings Pomering, 1995, Ellicott City, Maryland, 64½" x 79½". (Quilted by Marcia Stevens)*

Meet the Teacher

Connie Stillings Pomering fell in love with quilts at an early age and caught the quilting bug while living near an Amish community. Her early love of wide borders, simple patterns, and vibrant colors has not wavered. Connie discovered rotary cutting and machine piecing in 1984. But these finds were soon rivaled by her discovery in 1987 of machine quilting. Now those tops that were piling up could be finished and eventually grace her walls and beds.

Among Connie's favorite quilts are Log Cabin, Kaleidoscope, Roman Stripe, Tumbling Blocks, and Trip Around the World. She likes to work with variations of the traditional repeat block quilt, and she has enormous respect for the quilters who came before us.

Connie has been playing with the Strip-Pieced Log Cabin block since 1991. While making pre-pieced strip sets for a Kaleidoscope quilt, she discovered there were endless possibilities for using presewn logs in a variety of Log Cabin blocks and settings. The quilts pictured here are only two examples of how the blocks can be arranged to create exciting quilts. Connie finds great joy in being able to turn a simple block into a quilt that stops someone in their tracks!

Teaching is something Connie also enjoys. She is constantly amazed by her students' work, most of which is done in precious moments between juggling full-time families, homes, and jobs. It is a testimony to the need in all of us to create, she says.

TEACHER'S QUILT:
Razzmatazz
*by Connie Stillings Pomering, 1995,
Ellicott City, Maryland, 63" x 63".
(Quilted by Marcia Stevens)*

Finished Quilt Size: 64½" x 79½"

SELECTING FABRICS

"The Wave" contains a multitude of prints and a single solid background fabric, while "Razzmatazz" contains only 2 prints (black and white) and several multicolor background prints.

To simplify the directions, only 6 fabrics are called for. Choose 1 fabric for the background—the unpieced strips. Choose 5 other fabrics in a gradation from light to dark. If the background fabric is dark, then fabric #1 should be the lightest fabric. If the background fabric is light, then fabric #1 should be the darkest fabric.

MATERIALS: *44"-wide fabric*

1⅝ yds. for background
1 yd. for fabric #1
⅞ yd. for fabric #2
⅝ yd. for fabric #3
½ yd. for fabric #4
⅓ yd. for fabric #5
⅝ yd. for inner border
2⅜ yds. for outer border (cut on the lengthwise grain)
4¾ yds. for backing (pieced lengthwise)
⅞ yd. for bias binding
68" x 83" piece of thin batting

CUTTING

Cut all strips across the width of the fabric (crosswise grain) unless otherwise indicated.

From the background fabric, cut:

3 strips, each 2" x 42"
3 strips, each 3½" x 42"
3 strips, each 5" x 42"
3 strips, each 6½" x 42"

From fabric #1, cut:

15 strips, each 2" x 42"

From fabric #2, cut:

12 strips, each 2" x 42"

From fabric #3, cut:

9 strips, each 2" x 42"

From fabric #4, cut:

6 strips, each 2" x 42"

From fabric #5, cut:

3 strips, each 2" x 42"

From the inner-border fabric, cut:

6 strips, each 2½" x 42"

From the lengthwise grain *of the outer-border fabric, cut:*

2 strips, each 8" x 49½", for top and bottom borders
2 strips, each 8" x 79½", for side borders

ASSEMBLING THE BLOCKS

Finished Block Size: 7½" x 7½"

Tip Accurate cutting, careful pressing (an often over-looked step), and sewing with an accurate ¼"-wide seam allowance will ensure that your blocks finish to the correct size and fit together well. It is a good idea to use the same sewing machine throughout the piecing project, to ensure that your seam allowances do not vary.

1. Sew strips together as shown to make 3 each of strip sets A–E. Press seams as indicated by the arrows. Cut a total of 48 segments, each 2" wide, from each of strip sets A–E. Save the remainder of the strip set in case you make an error in cutting or for another project.

Strip Set A

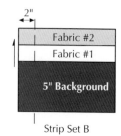

Strip Set B

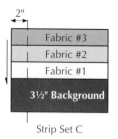

Strip Set C

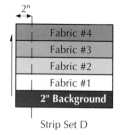

Strip Set D

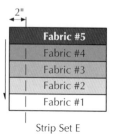

Strip Set E

2. Sew the segments together as shown to complete the block. Press the seams toward strip set A.

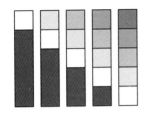 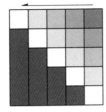

Make 48.

ASSEMBLING THE QUILT TOP & FINISHING

1. Arrange the blocks on your design wall, trying a variety of settings. Any of the traditional Log Cabin settings will work. To view your work from a distance, use a reducing glass, a door peephole from the hardware store, or the wrong end of a pair of binoculars. It will help you determine if the blocks are balanced. To make "The Wave," rotate the blocks as shown on page 40 to create the Streak of Lightning setting.

Tip: Use an instant camera to shoot all your setting options. It is eye-opening to see different settings side by side. Get your whole family involved. Husbands and children are amazingly frank and like to be included in your projects.

2. When you have decided on the best possible layout for your blocks (they will talk to you if you listen), chain-piece the blocks as shown. For each row, chain-piece the blocks in columns 1 and 2 together. Do not cut the threads between the rows. Join the blocks in columns 3 and 4, then the blocks in columns 5 and 6.

3. Sew column 1/2 to column 3/4, then add column 5/6. Before cutting the threads between the rows, mark the top left corner of the first block in each row to keep the rows from getting mixed up. Put 1 pin in row 1, 2 pins in row 2, and so on. Press the seams joining the blocks in opposite directions from row to row.

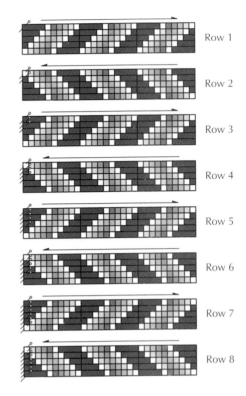

Row 1
Row 2
Row 3
Row 4
Row 5
Row 6
Row 7
Row 8

4. Join the rows, making sure to match the seams between the blocks.
5. Add 2½"-wide inner border strips (piecing as necessary) to the top and bottom edges first, then to the sides. Repeat with 8"-wide outer-border strips.
6. Layer the quilt top with batting and backing; baste.
7. Quilt as desired.
8. Bind the edges and label your quilt.

CHIMNEYS & CORNERSTONES

By Shirley Wolf

TEACHER'S QUILT: Chimneys and Cornerstones *by Shirley Wolf, Salina, Kansas, 1991, 93½" x 111½".*
(Quilted by Mary Jean Millikin)

Meet the Teacher

$\mathcal{S}$hirley Wolf took her first quilting class in 1981 at the Quilting Bee in Salina, Kansas. She purchased the shop in 1984 and now teaches many of its classes, in addition to lecturing and teaching throughout Kansas and surrounding states. She enjoys teaching all aspects of quilting, including finishing techniques and the care and storage of antique quilts. Shirley has been responsible for starting many beginners on the road to a happy quilting life.

Shirley's interests vary from hand appliqué to machine quilting. It is her dream to be known for her effective use of color in traditional as well as contemporary quilt patterns.

The inspiration for "Chimneys and Cornerstones" came from a picture of an antique quilt. Using contemporary fabrics from The Quilting Bee's shelves, Shirley brought the antique to life. She taught her first Chimneys and Cornerstones class in 1991, but it wasn't until she was asked to present an educational display at the Salina Silver Needles Guild Show in 1994 that the top was quilted. Shirley then offered the class again.

Phylis Smith, the maker of the purple Chimneys and Cornerstones quilt, started quilting in March 1995. As of October 1, 1995, she had taken eleven classes at The Quilting Bee, eight of which were for full-sized quilts. Phylis also finished several other small projects during this same time. How proud can you be of a student!

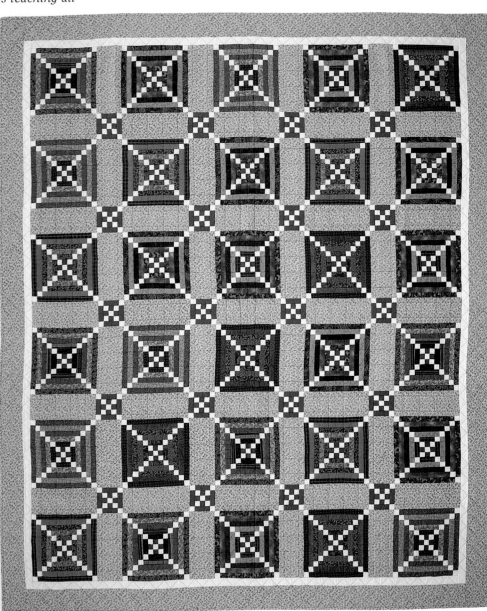

STUDENT'S QUILT: Purple Corners
*by Phylis Smith, 1995,
Salina, Kansas, 93½" x 111½".*

Finished Quilt Size: 93½" x 111½"

Use stripes, plaids, and small old-fashioned prints.

½ yd. each of 8 to 10 dark tan-and-black prints for the main block

½ yd. each of 6 to 8 medium tan-and-black prints for the main block

2⅔ yds. light tan solid for cornerstones, center nine-patch unit, posts, and inner border

⅜ yd. rust for center nine-patch unit

¾ yd. black print for posts

3¾ yds. medium tan print for sashing and outer border

10 yds. for backing (pieced lengthwise)

120" x 120" piece of very low-loft batting

1 yd. black-and-tan check for binding

$\mathcal{C}$UTTING

Chimneys and Cornerstones Blocks

Before cutting, sort the medium and dark tan-and-black prints into 6 groups of 5 fabrics each, starting and ending with a dark. Label the fabrics as shown. Use a fabric more than once within the 6 groups.

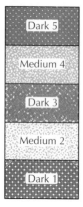
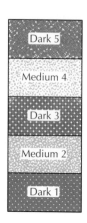

Group 1   Group 2

Sort into 6 groups.

From each group of sorted fabrics, cut 1 each of the following strips:

Dark 1	3½" x 42"
Medium 2	5½" x 42"
Dark 3	7½" x 42"
Medium 4	9½" x 42"
Dark 5	11½" x 42"

Cut each strip in half to yield 2 strips, each 21" long.

From the light tan solid, cut:

7 strips, each 1½" x 42", for center nine-patch units; cut 1 strip in half to yield 2 strips, each 21" long.

30 strips, each 1½" x 42"; cut each strip in half to yield 2 strips, each 21" long, for a total of 60 strips

From the rust print, cut:

6 strips, each 1½" x 42", for the center nine-patch units; cut 1 strip in half to yield 2 strips, each 21" long

Posts

From the light tan solid, cut:

9 strips, each 1½" x 42", for nine-patch units

From the black print, cut:

4 strips, each 1½" x 42", for nine-patch units

4 strips, each 3½" x 42", for framing

Sashing, Borders, and Binding

From the light tan solid, cut:

10 strips, each 2" x 42", for inner borders

From the medium tan print, cut:

7 strips, each 13½" x 42"; crosscut into 49 rectangles, each 5½" x 13½", for sashing

10 strips, each 3" x 42", for outer borders

From the black-and-tan check, cut:

11 strips, 3" x 42", for binding

ASSEMBLING THE CHIMNEYS & CORNERSTONES BLOCKS

Finished Block Size: 13" x 13"

1. Sew 1½" x 42" light tan and rust strips together as shown to make 2 Strip Units A and 1 Strip Unit B. Press the seams toward the rust. Sew the 1½" x 21" light tan and rust strips together in the same manner to make 1 Strip Unit A and 1 Strip Unit B. Cut a total of 60 segments, each 1½" wide, from Strip Units A. Cut a total of 30 segments, each 1½" wide, from Strip Unit B.

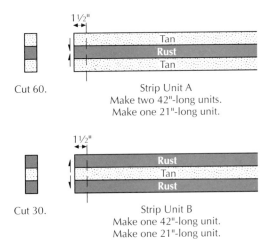

Cut 60.

Strip Unit A
Make two 42"-long units.
Make one 21"-long unit.

Cut 30.

Strip Unit B
Make one 42"-long unit.
Make one 21"-long unit.

2. Join the segments as shown to make nine-patch units. Press the seams away from the center segment. Make a total of 30 nine-patch units.

3. Working with one group of sorted strips at a time, sew a 1½" x 21" light tan strip to opposite sides of each strip in the group.

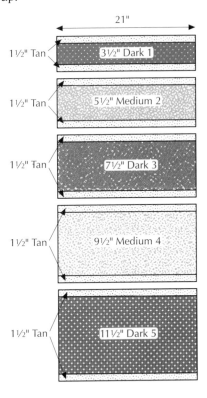

4. Stack the 5 strip units on top of each other with the Dark 1 strip unit on top and Dark 5 at the bottom as shown. Straighten the left edge, and cut 10 segments, each 1½" wide, from the stacked strip units.

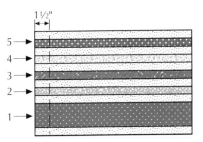

Leaving the cut segments stacked, arrange the stacks in pairs, 1 pair for each block.

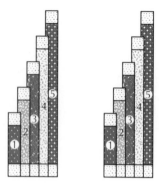

Pieced strips stacked for 1 block

5. Stack the remaining 21"-long tan-and-black strips as shown. Straighten the left edge and cut 10 segments, each 1½" wide, from the stack.

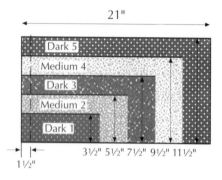

Add 2 stacks of strips to each pair of segments set aside for the blocks.

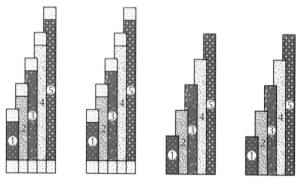

Stacked strips for 1 block

6. Repeat steps 3 and 4 with each of the remaining 5 groups of fabric strips. When you've completed the piecing and cutting for all 6 groups of fabric, you should have stacks of strips to make 30 blocks.

7. Working with the strips for 1 block at a time, assemble the strips around a center nine-patch unit as shown. Starting with the Dark 1 strips, add the unpieced strips to opposite sides first, then add the matching pieced strips to the adjacent sides. Add the strips for remaining rounds

in order, ending with Dark 5 for the last round. Press all seams away from the center nine-patch unit.

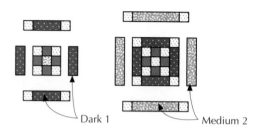

Make 30.

ASSEMBLING THE POSTS

Finished Block Size: 5" x 5"

1. Sew the 1½" x 42" light tan solid and black print strips together as shown to make 2 Strip Unit A and 1 Strip Unit B. Press the seams toward the black print. Cut a total of 40 segments, each 1½" wide, from Strip Unit A. Cut 20 segments, each 1½" wide, from Strip Unit B.

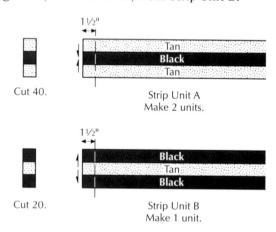

2. Join the segments as shown to make 1 nine-patch unit. Press the seams away from the center segment. Make a total of 20 nine-patch units.

3. Sew a 1½" x 42" light tan solid strip to each side of a 3½" x 42" black print strip to make 2 identical strip units. Cut a total of 40 segments, each 1½" wide, from the strip units.

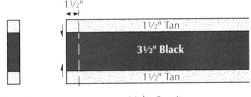

Cut 40.   Make 2 units.

4. Cut a total of 40 segments, each 1½" wide, from the remaining 3½"-wide black print strips.

Cut 40.

5. Frame a nine-patch unit with the segments cut in steps 3 and 4 to make 1 Post block as shown. Press the seams away from the center unit. Make a total of 20 Post blocks.

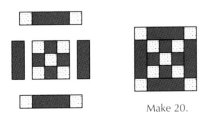

Make 20.

ASSEMBLING THE QUILT TOP & FINISHING

1. Sew the blocks and 5½" x 13½" sashing strips together as shown to make 6 identical rows. Press the seams toward the sashing strips.

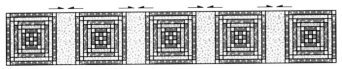

Make 6.

2. Sew the Post blocks and remaining sashing strips together as shown to make 5 identical rows. Press the seams toward the sashing strips.

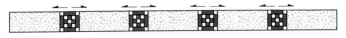

Make 5.

3. Sew the rows and sashing together as shown, taking care to match all seams.

4. Add the 2"-wide inner-border strips to the sides first, seaming strips as necessary, then to the top and bottom edges. Repeat with 3"-wide outer-border strips.
5. Layer the quilt top with batting and backing; baste.
6. Quilt as desired. Shirley quilted a 1" straight grid across the quilt following the strips of the basic block, and a 1" diagonal grid in the borders.
7. Bind the edges and label your quilt.

LATTICE DESIGNS

By Wendy Hill

Karen & Wendy

Meet the Teacher

*W*endy Hill often starts her classes by introducing herself and her alter ego, Ratty, a foot-long rat doll with a bright orange tongue and turquoise tail. Ratty is not what she appears to be: turn her inside out and she becomes a tote bag. Wendy, like Ratty, reveals her flip side in classes. She is knowledgeable yet offbeat and imaginative. If Wendy could give her students just one thing, it would be belief in their own abilities. When a person makes a quilt with an authentic voice, the quilt becomes more than the sum of materials, Wendy says.

While developing a proposal for church banners, Wendy thought of an easy way to get a stained-glass look. A trial run worked, and the resulting set of four two-sided banners now hanging in their sanctuary look more like illuminated stained glass than pieced fabric quilts.

She quickly saw the potential for making quilts ranging from stained glass designs to garden paths, and developed a class so quilters could make beautiful one- and two-sided quilts.

One of Wendy's students, Karen Laux, began quilting after she and her husband retired. Convinced she wouldn't care for the enormous amount of time and effort that goes into quilt-making, she agreed to make one block. Of course, one block led to another and another, until within a short time Karen had received two ribbons for her quilts.

Wendy, a studio-art quilter, and author, lives in Sunriver, Oregon.

TEACHER'S QUILT
Inner Rhythms and Chaotic Harmonies I
by Wendy Hill, 1994, Sunriver, Oregon 60" x 44"

STUDENT'S QUILT:
Broken Glass
*by Karen Laux, 1995,
Downieville, California,
17¾" x 21½".*

Design option based on "Lattice Scene II" by Wendy Hill. This is a two-sided banner designed to hang between Wendy's kitchen and dining room. She prequilted the window fabric on both sides to add texture.

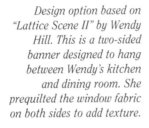

Design option based on "Scatterings," a two-sided quilt by Page Alexander. Page wanted to depict a stone path in a garden. Brown lattice fabric represents dirt (fall) on one side and green lattice fabric represents grass (spring) on the other. Page prequilted the window fabrics and embellished both sides with found objects such as leaves, petals, and acorns.

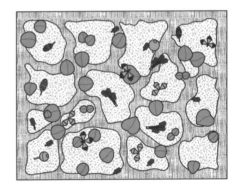

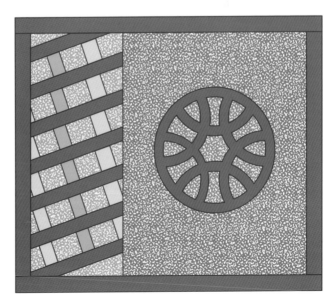

Design option based on "Untitled 9,999" by Fran Andre. Fran used hand-painted canvas for the background and a simplified Celtic design for the lattice.

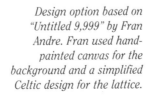

THE BIG PICTURE

Instead of copying a specific project, you will learn how to use a technique to make your own one- or two-sided quilts or banners. The technique is broken down into five easy steps.

1. Assembling the quilt sandwich.
2. Marking the lattice design.
3. Sewing along the marked lines with a small, straight stitch.
4. Cutting away the excess lattice fabric after all the lines have been sewn to reveal the window fabric.
5. Zigzagging the edges of the lattice fabric through all the layers.

That's all there is to it. In five easy steps, you have a beautiful piece that looks far more complicated than it really is. Any design with lattice strips can be adapted for use with this technique. The quilt or banner can look like stained glass as in "Inner Rhythms and Chaotic Harmonies" on pages 50–51, or you can try less conventional ideas, such as a stone path in a garden, illustrated on page 51.

The terms "window fabric" and "window panel" refer to the fabric that is under or behind the lattice or "lead." In a stained-glass design, the window fabric is the "glass," and the lattice is the lead.

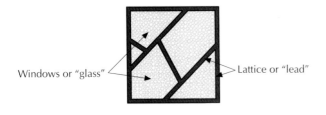

Windows or "glass"   Lattice or "lead"

GATHERING MATERIALS

Fabric

In general, the selected fabrics must be compatible with the end use. Consider lightfastness when selecting fabric, since these pieces are meant to hang and might fade over time. Tightly woven fabrics or other fabrics resistant to raveling are good choices for the lattice. Fiber content is less important since these wall hangings and banners are not machine washed.

Look for fabrics with high contrast in color and texture. If the contrast between the lattice strips and the window fabric is not great enough, the design will be lost. Fabrics that appear solid from a distance are good choices for lattices. If you want the look of stained glass, use saturated colors for the windows and a dark or black fabric for the lattice.

Until you gain experience with fabric selection, it is a good idea to make a sample before committing yourself to the entire project. Make a mock-up by gluing fabrics on paper or fusing to fusible interfacing. Hang the mock-up on a wall and view it close up as well as from a distance.

Thread

Use cotton, polyester, or cotton-polyester blend thread to match the lattice fabric. It is important for the thread to blend in, so avoid rayon, metallic, or other specialty threads that reflect light or draw attention to themselves. If matching thread is unavailable, try clear or smoky monofilament thread.

Middle Layer

Choose muslin, flannel, or batting for the middle layer. Flannel and muslin give a compact look and add weight, allowing the piece to hang flat and straight. For a softer look with some loft, use a low-loft cotton, polyester, or cotton-polyester blend batting.

Walking Foot

A walking foot is preferable to a regular presser foot when sewing through several layers, with or without batting.

SELECTING A DESIGN

You can draft an original design, adapt a design, or use a design from books with no copyright restrictions. Look for designs in which the lattice is at least ¼" wide and the same color throughout. When making a two-sided project, remember the design is reversed on the back. The design should be simple enough to follow with your sewing machine foot (regular or walking foot).

The following books, all published by Dover Publications, Inc., are good resources for copyright-free designs: *Chinese Lattice Designs* and *The New Book of Chinese Lattice Designs* by Daniel Sheets Dye and *Handbook of Designs and Devices* by Clarence P. Hornung.

The design you select may need to be enlarged. The easiest way is to use a photocopy machine; however, this can be expensive when oversized paper is required. Another method is to use an opaque or overhead projector. (Use opaque projectors with designs on paper; use overhead projectors with designs on acetate or clear plastic.) Project the enlarged image on a wall, then trace it onto paper. Both projectors can be purchased or are often available to rent from libraries and quilt shops.

PLANNING

You can use the following options and the five basic steps to make individual blocks or a wall hanging. You can construct your project in the usual manner, sewing together individual blocks, sashing, and borders; layering with batting and backing; then quilting. Or you can layer, stitch together, and quilt all at once, as was done with "Inner Rhythms and Chaotic Harmonies II" (page 50) and "Broken Glass"(page 51).

Although the same five steps are used with all projects, there are choices that need to be determined before starting. Review this section as you plan your project.

One or Two Sides

One-sided pieces hang on a wall, and have the advantage of using less fabric. Two-sided pieces can hang on a wall (with only one side showing at a time) or in an open space (with both sides exposed).

A two-sided quilt or banner allows you to play with color schemes, fabric assortments, and looks. The two sides could reflect opposites in the seasons (spring/summer versus fall/winter), decorating schemes (country versus modern), or moods (vibrant versus somber).

Window-Fabric Variations

You can use whole cloth, including hand-dyed or painted panels, pieced panels, or individually placed pieces for the windows. The easiest choice is one piece of fabric. The size of the finished quilt will be limited by the width of the fabric unless two or more pieces of fabric are sewn together. Look for fabrics with irregular designs for more variety. For a unique piece, consider painted, dyed, or airbrushed fabrics.

Piecing a window panel is another choice. Keep it simple or make it complicated. Try strip piecing, piecing one template shape (triangles, squares, hexagons, or other shapes), or using a repeat block design. "Inner Rhythms and Chaotic Harmonies" is made of triangle shapes.

To Quilt or Not to Quilt

It is not necessary to quilt the window fabric to the middle layer; however, quilting can add another design element to your finished piece. The quilting is done before the sandwich is made. Quilting adds weight and stiffness, which helps the quilt or banner hang straight and flat.

One-sided pieces have a backing, a middle layer, window fabric, and lattice fabric. To quilt the window fabric, layer it with batting (or flannel or muslin) and an additional layer of muslin. Baste or pin the layers, and quilt using monofilament or colored thread. After quilting, continue with Step One, layering the quilted fabric with the backing and lattice fabric.

Two-sided pieces have lattice fabric, window fabric, a middle layer, window fabric, and lattice fabric. To quilt the window fabrics, layer each one with batting (or flannel or muslin) and muslin; baste and quilt as above. If both window fabrics are quilted, there will be two middle layers for each side. Continue with Step One, layering the quilted fabrics with the backing and lattice fabrics.

Finishing the Edges

There are two options for both one- and two-sided quilts.

Option 1: Finish the edges with a double-fold French binding. This is a good method to use when the binding will add to the color and design of the quilt or banner.

Option 2: Finish the edges with a pillowcase lining before Step One. This method is preferable when the addition of a binding would interfere with the overall lattice design. Some lattice designs already include a strip around the edges of the design.

- For a one-sided design, stack the middle layer, window fabric (right side up), and lattice fabric (right side up). Place the backing and lattice fabrics right sides together; hand baste to keep the layers from shifting. Stitch around the edges with a ¼"-wide seam allowance, leaving an opening for turning. Clip the corners and trim batting to reduce bulk.

Leave open for turning.

Turn right side out and hand stitch the opening closed. Press and baste to hold the layers together. Continue with Step Two.

- For a two-sided design, stack the window fabric (right side down), middle layer, window fabric (right side up), and lattice fabric (right side up). When using the same lattice fabric on the front and back, put a small piece of masking tape on the front panel of the lattice fabric. In Step Two, you will mark the lattice design on this side. Place the lattice fabric for the back right sides together with the lattice fabric for the front. Stitch, trim, and turn as described above for a one-sided design.

One-Sided Quilt

Hang one-sided quilts as you would any other, with a casing (sleeve), rings, or clamps.

Casing

1. The casing should be 3" to 6" wide, and 1" to 2" shorter than the width of the quilt. Fold the ends under ½", then under ½" again, and stitch. Fold the fabric strip in half lengthwise, right sides together, and sew a ¼"- to ½"-wide seam. Press the seam open and turn the tube inside out so the seam is centered on one side.

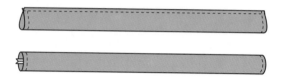

2. Center the casing ½" to 1" below and parallel to the top edge, and ½" to 1" from each side. Hand stitch the top and bottom edges.

Quilt back

3. Insert a dowel or a flat board through the casing (drill holes through the ends first) and hang by monofilament thread.

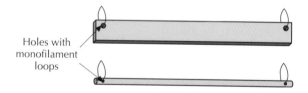

Holes with monofilament loops

Rings

Hand stitch small plastic rings (available at most fabric stores in the notions department) at 8" to 12" intervals parallel to and just below the top edge of the quilt. Pin thumb tacks through the rings to hang the quilt.

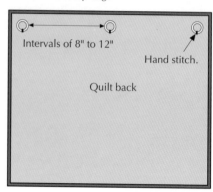

½" to 1" from top edge

Intervals of 8" to 12"

Hand stitch.

Quilt back

Clamps

You can buy decorative clamps at quilt shops or from catalogs. Mount the clamps on the wall, following the manufacturer's instructions.

Two-Sided Quilt

A different method is needed to hang two-sided quilts, since both sides need to be free of casings or rings. The easiest method is to hang the quilt from fabric loops spaced at 8" to 12" intervals along the top edge. Make the loops from the lattice or binding fabric so they complement the quilt.

When using binding, slip the loops under the binding, catching them when you stitch the binding. Topstitch loops in place along the top edge of the binding.

Intervals of 8" to 12"

Quilt front

Slip loops under the binding and stitch.

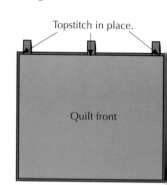

Topstitch in place.

Quilt front

When using the pillowcase lining method, include the loops in the seam (reinforce this seam with double stitching). When turned right side out, the tabs will extend out of the seam along the top edge.

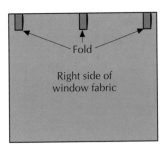

Right side of
window fabric

Fold

Wrong side of
window fabric

Quilt front

To hang, insert a dowel through the tabs and hang with monofilament thread as described for a one-sided quilt.

$\mathcal{A}$SSEMBLING THE QUILT

Using the checklist in "Planning," decide which options you will choose, then follow the five steps described below.

Step One: Making the Sandwich

Stack the layers in the order indicated below for the type of quilt you are making. Baste the layers together with thread in lines about 4" apart; safety pins are not practical with this technique. It is important to baste horizontally, vertically, and diagonally so the layers are held together firmly. A little extra time at this stage will make the resulting quilt or banner look professional.

Individual Blocks
    Muslin
    Window fabric (right side up)
    Lattice fabric (right side up)
One-Sided Quilt
    Backing (right side down)
    Middle layer
    Window fabric (right side up)
    Lattice fabric (right side up)
Two-Sided Quilt
    Lattice fabric (right side down)
    Window fabric (right side down)
    Middle layer
    Window fabric (right side up)
    Lattice fabric (right side up)

Step Two: Marking the Lattice Design

Mark the lattice design on the right side of the lattice fabric. The marking method depends on personal preference, the size of the project, and the lattice fabric.

Transfer Pen: Use an iron-on transfer pen to transfer your design to the lattice fabric. These permanent-ink pens are available in many colors. Use the pen to trace over the design. Place the ink side down on the lattice fabric. Following the manufacturer's directions, use a hot iron (place and press, don't slide and glide) to transfer the design to the lattice fabric. The transferred image is the mirror image of the drawing.

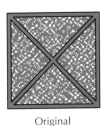

Original   Copy

Symmetrical designs are identical.

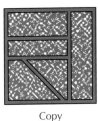

Original   Copy

Asymmetrical designs are mirror images.

For projects larger than the ironing board, Wendy moves the iron to a large table. The entire quilt is flat on the surface and doesn't need to be moved while ironing.

Pros and Cons: This method is good for most projects, especially large pieces and designs with curvy lines. The ink may be transferred several times with one inking, an advantage for a project with repeated images. One drawback is that the ink may show on the lattice fabric. The ink is permanent and, on some fabrics, may remain visible after sewing and zigzagging. Test the ink on a scrap of lattice fabric before using.

Freezer Paper: Freezer paper is waxy on one side. It is sold in grocery stores in the plastic-wrap and bag section. Trace the design onto the uncoated side. Using a warm iron, press the waxy side onto the lattice fabric. Hold the paper in place with a few pins around the edges and at the corners to prevent it from peeling off while you sew. Stitch on the lines with a small stitch length, then remove the freezer paper.

Pros and Cons: This inexpensive method is good for designs with curvy lines and works best with small projects. Large projects require rolling and more handling when sewing the lines, and the freezer paper tends to peel off while you maneuver the piece through the sewing machine. Prevent this by holding the freezer paper in place with safety pins.

Stitch-n-Tear: This tear-away product by Pellon® works much like freezer paper. Trace the design onto the Stitch-n-Tear. Thread- or pin-baste it in place on the lattice fabric. Sew on the lines, using a small stitch length, then remove the Stitch-n-Tear.

Pros and Cons: This is a good option for most projects, especially larger designs and those with curvy lines. Since it must be basted in place, however, it adds more time to the construction process.

Step Three: Sewing on the Lines

Stitch along the lines through *all* layers of the one- or two-sided project. Always use thread to match the lattice fabric. Set the stitch length smaller than normal, about 12 to 14 stitches per inch or 2.0 to 2.5 for computerized machines. Use a backstitch at the beginning and end of each line of stitching. Clip thread ends close to the fabric surface. A walking foot is advisable for two-sided projects and for projects with batting. Stitch around each of the shapes within your design as shown. Do not stitch across the lattice lines.

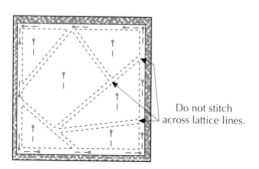

Do not stitch across lattice lines.

Tip Larger projects need to be packaged for easier handling. Roll the sides and clip with quilting clamps. Accordion-fold the piece into your lap and allow it to flow through the machine. Do not allow the quilt to hang by its own weight off the side of the table or your lap. With proper support for the quilt, it will be easier to control the stitching.

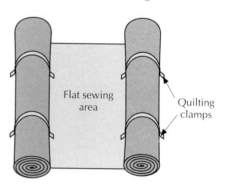

Flat sewing area

Quilting clamps

Step Four: Revealing the Windows

Cutting away the excess lattice fabric to reveal the windows is similar to reverse appliqué. Any type of scissors may be used, although many people have a preference. Experiment to find which is right for you and the project

1. To cut away the excess lattice fabric covering the window fabric, pinch the lattice fabric and pull it away from the window fabric below it. Make sure only the lattice fabric is being pinched. Cut a small slit in the pinched fabric.

Pinch.

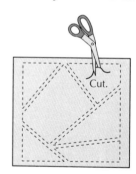

Cut.

2. Insert the point of the scissors into the slit and cut across the fabric to 1/16" from the stitching line.

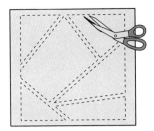

3. Cut around the shape, continuing to cut 1/16" from the stitching line until the window fabric is revealed.

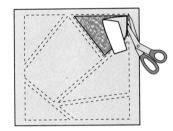

4. Continue cutting away the lattice fabric until all the windows are revealed. For two-sided projects, cut away all the excess lattice fabric on both sides before continuing with the Step Five. If you discover the lattice fabric is raveling more than you like, zigzag the windows as you go (see Step Five).

As you experiment with different designs, you may discover that leaving some windows covered adds to the power and impact of the overall design. It is not required to reveal all the windows, nor must you reveal the same windows on the front as on the back.

You may want to use the cut-out window shapes elsewhere in your quilt, as Karen Laux did in "Broken Glass." Instead of using the actual cutouts, cut new window shapes from extra lattice fabric. Trace the design onto freezer paper, cut out the window templates, lightly iron the templates onto the lattice fabric, and cut out. Use the same zigzag setting to apply the shapes where desired.

Step Five: Zigzagging the Edges

Set the sewing machine for a zigzag stitch. Use the same matching thread used in Step Three. Experiment on a scrap of lattice fabric to find the right width and closeness of the zigzag stitch. The width should be set so the zigzag crosses the stitching line to the cut edge. The zigzag stitches need to be close together, but slightly open. Do not use a satin stitch, in which the zigzags are packed next to each other.

Close together, but
slightly open

Start anywhere along the stitching line; my preference is near a corner. Bring up the bobbin thread, then backstitch or stitch in place a few times. Follow the stitching line so the zigzag falls just over the cut edge and crosses the stitching line. Overlap the starting place by 1 or 2 stitches, then finish with a backstitch or stitch in place a few times. Repeat on all the cut edges.

Zigzag crosses over the cut
edge and the stitching line.

FINISHING

At this point, both one- and two-sided quilts have either been finished with the pillowcase method or will require binding.

1. To bind your quilt, use a double-fold French binding or your favorite method. In the Planning stage (page 53), think about how wide you want the finished binding. For a wide binding, allow extra batting (or other middle layer) to extend beyond the edges. Or make a narrower binding equal to the width of the seam allowance (1/4" to 1/2") used to attach the binding. Fold the binding to the back of the quilt and hand stitch.
2. Add rings or a sleeve if you did not add loops for hanging.
3. Sign or label your quilt. For two-sided quilts, sign your name along one edge with a metallic, permanent-ink pen.

1930s BASKET QUILT

By Beverly Dunivent

Meet the Teacher

*B*everly Dunivent has been making quilts since the late 1970s and teaching quiltmaking since 1979. She is a well-known quilt historian, having done extensive research on 1930s quilts and quilts made from kits. In addition to teaching and lecturing for guilds, stores, and quilting retreats throughout the United States, she restores quilts and teaches quilt restoration. Beverly is also a quilt appraiser certified by the American Quilter's Society.

Beverly's love affair with 1930s quilts began when she received a Double Wedding Ring quilt from her mother. Her mother started the quilt in 1927 and finished it in the early 1950s. After receiving the quilt, Beverly decided it would be fun to make quilts with the look of the 1930s using today's techniques.

Her inspiration for "1930s Basket Quilt" came from antique Stamp Basket quilts. Beverly used fabric scraps from her vintage collection as well as reproduction fabrics. She updated the construction of the quilt to take advantage of rotary-cutting and quick-sewing techniques. She even simplified the handle, making it straight rather than curved.

Judy Raynesford was a student in a class Beverly taught at Creative Expressions, a quilt shop in Palm Springs. Judy has decorated the guest bedroom of her home with the 1930s look. Her Basket quilt complements a Pansy kit quilt on the bed and nostalgic pieces in the room.

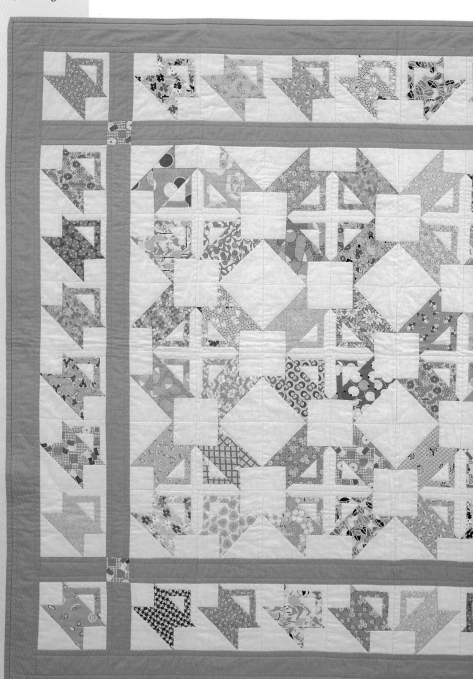

STUDENT'S QUILT:
1930s Basket Quilt
by Judy Raynesford, 1995,
Palm Springs California,
50½" x 61½".

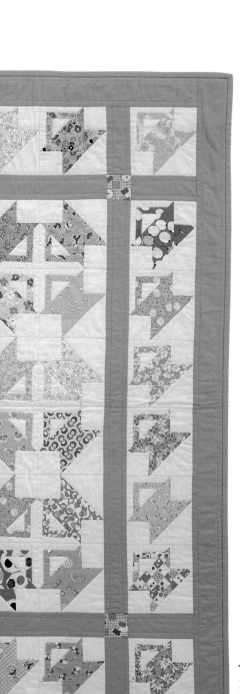

TEACHER'S QUILT:
1930s Basket Quilt
by Beverly Dunivent, 1995,
Green Valley Lake, California,
53½" x 64".

Finished Quilt Size: 64½" x 53½"

$\mathcal{M}$ATERIALS: 44"-wide fabric

2 yds. off-white or muslin for background
1¾ yds. total assorted vintage or reproduction 1930s prints
   (fat eighths and fat quarters work well)
2 yds. reproduction 1930s green solid for lattice, borders, and
   binding
3⅜ yds. for backing (pieced lengthwise)
62" x 72" piece of cotton batting
½" or 12mm Bias Maker (optional)

$\mathcal{C}$UTTING

From the background fabric, cut:

9 strips, each 4½" x 42"; crosscut into 80 squares, each 4½"
   x 4½". Cut squares once diagonally to yield 160 triangles: 80 for piece 1 and 80 for piece 5.
10 strips, each 2⅜" x 42"; crosscut into 160 squares, each 2⅜"
   x 2⅜", for piece 3

From the assorted 1930s prints, cut a total of:

40 squares, each 4½" x 4½"; cut squares once diagonally to
   yield 80 triangles for piece 2
80 squares, each 2¾" x 2¾"; cut squares once diagonally to
   yield 160 triangles for piece 4
80 strips, each 1" x 6", for handles
4 squares, each 2½" x 2½", for cornerstones

   NOTE: Each basket requires 2 small triangles, 1 large
   triangle, and 1 handle cut from the same fabric.

From the lengthwise grain of the 1930s green, cut:

2 strips, each 2½" x 33½"
2 strips, each 2½" x 44½"
8 strips, each 2½" x 6"
2 strips, each 3" x 64½", for outer top and bottom borders
2 strips, each 3" x 48½", for outer side borders
6 strips, each 2½" x 62", for binding

$\mathcal{A}$SSEMBLING THE BLOCKS

Finished Block Size: 5½" x 5½"

Use the same print for all the components of each basket.

1. To form a basket handle, use the Bias Maker to turn over
   the long edges ¼" on each 1" x 6" print strip. If you don'
   have a Bias Marker, fold both the long edges over ¼" (wrong
   sides together) so the raw edges meet in the middle.

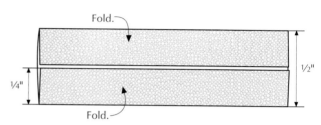

2. With a pencil, draw a line ¾" from the 2 short edges of a
   piece 1 background triangle.

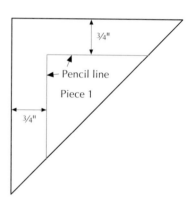

3. Position the handle along the drawn line, just covering
   the line. Make a 45° fold at the corner. Stitch ¹/₁₆" from the
   edge along both sides of the handle. Trim the ends even
   with the edge of the triangle.

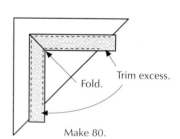

Make 80.

4. Assemble the pieces as shown to complete a Basket block. The block should measure 5½" square. Square up the edges if necessary.

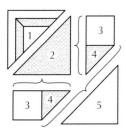 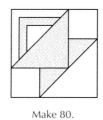

Make 80.

ASSEMBLING THE QUILT TOP & FINISHING

1. Arrange 48 Basket blocks for the center, referring to the photo on page 58. Sew 4 blocks together, basket handles all facing inward, to make a large block.

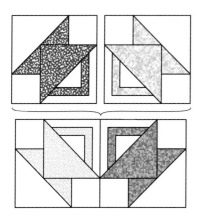

2. Sew the large blocks together in horizontal rows. Press the seams in opposite directions from row to row, then join the rows.

3. Sew the 2½" x 33½" green strips to the sides of the quilt top. Add a 2½" print square to each end of the 2½" x 44½" green strips. Sew these to the top and bottom edges.

4. Join 6 Basket blocks for each of the side borders. Add a 2½" x 6" green strip to each end of the row of basket blocks. Sew these to the sides of the quilt top.

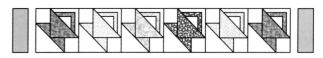

Side Borders
Make 2.

5. Join 8 Basket blocks and two 2½" x 6" green strips as shown to make the top and bottom borders. Sew these to the top and bottom edges of the quilt top.

Top and Bottom Borders
Make 2.

6. Add the 3" x 48½" green outer borders strips to the sides first, then add the 3" x 64½" green strips to the top and bottom edges.

7. Layer the quilt top with batting and backing; baste.

8. Quilt as desired. Beverly quilted in-the-ditch around each basket and along all the seam lines, and outline quilted ½" from both sides of the lattice and outer border seams.

9. Bind the edges and label your quilt.

ODE TO A CHRISTMAS TREE

By Lyn Mann

Teacher's Quilt: Ode to a Christmas Tree *by Lyn Mann, 1995, Lake Forest, California, 69" x 78". (Quilted by Teri Dowdee)*

Meet the Teacher

*B*orn and raised outside Cleveland, Ohio, Lyn Mann moved to California after graduating from Bowling Green State University. She took her first quilting class in 1981 and started teaching quilting classes in 1987.

She currently teaches at numerous quilt shops throughout southern California as well as teaches and lectures to guilds throughout the country. Lyn realized a dream come true in 1995 when she taught on a quilting cruise that traveled from the Canary Islands to Barbados.

Lyn is best known for her speed-pieced scrap quilts. During class, she does a great deal of one-on-one teaching, always sharing any little tricks she has learned over the years.

Lyn lives in Lake Forest, California, with her son, Damon.

Several years ago, Lyn turned her living room into a classroom, and that is where she met Kathleen Melikian. Kathleen started quilting in 1992 and credits Lyn with challenging her color horizons by always encouraging her to take risks.

Every year, Lyn creates a new Christmas quilt for a class. For Christmas 1995, she decided to use a Tree of Life block as the focal point. She added a variation of the Christmas Star block and the Chain block, using different background colors. It wasn't until after the blocks were all done and laid out that Lyn decided to turn the setting triangles into trees. Kathleen's quilt demonstrates how stunning the design can look when made up in different colors.

STUDENT'S QUILT: Winter Solstice
*by Kathleen Melikian, 1995,
Mission Viejo, California, 69" x 78".
(Quilted by Judi Tyrrell)*

Finished Quilt Size: 70⅞" x 79⅜"

MATERIALS: *44"-wide fabric*

⅜ yd. red check for center of dark star
1⅛ yds. green print for tree and star pieces
4⅛ yds. red print for star points, chain, and outer border
1¾ yds. for light background
2⅛ yds. for dark background
4⅞ yds. for backing (pieced lengthwise)
74" x 84" piece of batting
⅝ yd. for binding

DARK CHRISTMAS STAR BLOCKS

Finished Block Size: 6" x 6"

Cutting

From the red check, cut:

3 strips, each 3½"x 42"; crosscut strips into 32 squares, each 3½" x 3½"

From the green print, cut:

5 strips, each 1½" x 42"; crosscut strips into 128 squares, each 1½" x 1½"

From the red print, cut:

8 strips, each 2⅜" x 42"; crosscut strips into 128 squares, each 2⅜" x 2⅜". Cut the squares once diagonally to yield 256 triangles.

From the dark background, cut:

5 strips, each 2¾" x 42"; crosscut strips into 64 squares, each 2¾" x 2¾". Cut the squares twice diagonally to yield 256 triangles.
6 strips, each 2" x 42"; crosscut strips into 128 squares, each 2" x 2"

Assembly

1. Add a dark background triangle to 2 sides of a green square. Add a red print triangle to each of the short sides. The unit should measure 2" x 3½"; check your seam allowances if it does not. Press the seams toward the triangles. Make a total of 128 units.

Make 128.

2. To assemble the Christmas Star blocks, arrange 4 pieced units, 1 red check square, and 4 dark background squares as shown. Sew the units together in horizontal rows and press the seams in opposite directions as shown. Join the rows and press the seams toward the center row. Make a total of 32 dark blocks.

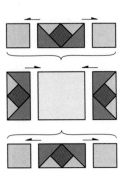 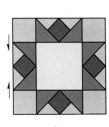

Make 32.

LIGHT CHRISTMAS STAR BLOCKS

Finished Block Size: 6" x 6"

Cutting

From the dark background, cut:

1 strip, 3½"x 42"; crosscut into 12 squares, each 3½" x 3½"

From green print, cut:

2 strips, each 1½" x 42"; crosscut strips into 48 squares, each 1½" x 1½"

From the red print, cut:

3 strips, each 2⅜" x 42"; crosscut strips into 48 squares, each 2⅜" x 2⅜". Cut the squares once diagonally to yield 96 triangles.

From the light background, cut:

2 strips, each 2¾" x 42"; crosscut strips into 24 squares, each 2¾" x 2¾". Cut the squares twice diagonally to yield 96 triangles.
3 strips, each 2" x 42"; crosscut strips into 48 squares, each 2" x 2"

Assembly

Follow steps 1 and 2 above to piece a light Christmas Star block. Use the light background pieces in place of the dark background pieces, and the 3½" dark background squares in place of the 3½" red check squares. Make 12 light blocks total.

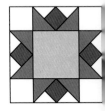

Make 12.

CHAIN BLOCKS

Finished Block Size: 6" x 6"

Cutting

From red print, cut:

3 strips, each 2½" x 42"; crosscut strips into 44 squares, each 2½" x 2½"
14 strips, each 1½" x 42"

From the light background, cut:

3 strips, each 2½" x 42"; crosscut strips into 48 squares, each 2½" x 2½"
4 strips, each 1½" x 42"

From the dark background, cut:

8 strips, each 2½" x 42"; crosscut strips into 128 squares, each 2½" x 2½"
10 strips, each 1½" x 42"

Assembly

1. Sew each dark background strip to a red strip. Press the seams toward the red. Cut a total of 256 segments, each 1½" wide, from the strip units. Sew each light background strip to a red strip. Press the seams toward the red. Cut a total of 96 segments, each 1½" wide, from the strip units.

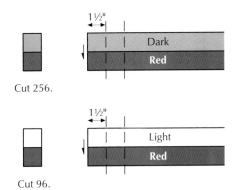

Cut 256.

Cut 96.

2. Assemble the four-patch units as shown. Press the seams to one side.

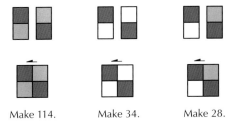

Make 114.   Make 34.   Make 28.

3. To assemble the Chain blocks, arrange the four-patch units and the light and dark background squares as shown. Sew the units together in horizontal rows and press the seams in opposite directions as shown. Join the rows and press the seams toward the center row. Make 44 blocks total.

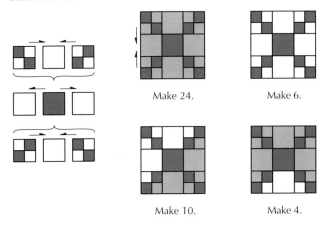

Make 24.   Make 6.

Make 10.   Make 4.

TREE OF LIFE BLOCK

Finished Block Size: 18" x 18"

Cutting

From the red print, cut:

1 square, 9⅞" x 9⅞"; cut the square once diagonally to yield 2 triangles (You will use only 1.)
1 strip, 1½" x 4¾", for the tree trunk
1 square, 3⅞" x 3⅞"; cut the square once diagonally to yield 2 triangles (You will use only 1.)

From the light background, cut:

1 square, 6¾" x 6¾"; cut the square once diagonally to yield 2 triangles
2 strips, each 3⅞" x 42"; crosscut strips into 12 squares, each 3⅞" x 3⅞"
3 squares, each 3½" x 3½"

From the green print, cut:

2 strips, each 3⅞" x 42"; crosscut strips into 12 squares, each 3⅞" x 3⅞"

Assembly

1. Sew a light triangle to each side of the 1½" x 4¾" red strip. Press the seams toward the red. Trim the ends of the triangles even with the end of the red strip as shown.

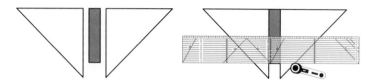

2. Sew a small red triangle to the base of the pieced unit. Sew a large red triangle to the opposite side.

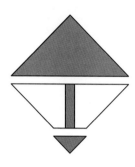

3. Draw a diagonal line from corner to corner on the back of each 3⅞" light square. Place a light square on top of a green square, right sides together. Stitch ¼" from the drawn line on both sides.

4. Cut on the drawn line. Press the seams toward the green, and trim the dog-ear corners. Each pair of squares yields 2 half-square triangle units. Make a total of 24 half-square triangle units.

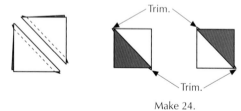

Trim.
Trim.
Make 24.

5. Arrange 9 half-square triangle units in 3 rows of 3 units each as shown. Sew the units in horizontal rows. Join the rows. Press the seams toward the bottom. Make 2 sections.

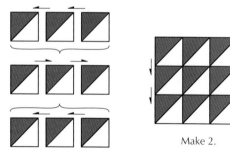

Make 2.

6. Arrange 6 half-square triangle units and 3 light background squares as shown. Sew the units in horizontal rows. Join the rows. Press the seams toward the bottom. Make 1 section.

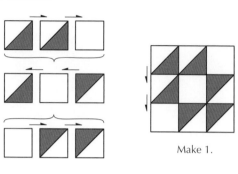

Make 1.

7. To assemble the Tree of Life block, arrange the sections as shown. Sew the sections together in pairs. Press the seams in opposite directions. Join the pairs to complete the block.

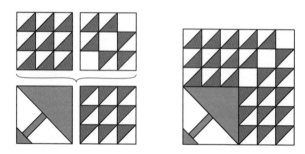

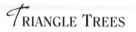

TRIANGLE TREES

Finished Block Size: 6" x 6" x 8½"

Cutting

From the green print, cut:

2 strips, each 7¼" x 42"; crosscut strips into 8 squares, each 7¼" x 7¼". Cut the squares twice diagonally to yield 32 triangles. (You will use only 30.)

From the red print, cut:

2 strips, each 1¾" x 42"; crosscut strips into 30 rectangles, each 1½" x 1¾"

From the light background, cut:

6 strips, each 1¾" x 42"

Assembly

1. Fold the light background strips in half crosswise; cut off the selvages. Measure 4⅝" from the left and make a small mark on the bottom edge of the strip.

Trim selvages.

2. Align the 45° angle line on your ruler with the bottom edge of the strip so the edge of the ruler is aligned with the mark. Cut along the edge of the ruler. This is your first set of trapezoids.

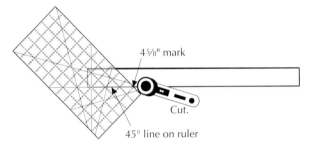

4⅝" mark

Cut.

45° line on ruler

3. To cut the next pair of trapezoids, measure 4⅝" from the top left point and make a mark at the top of the strip. Make a straight cut at this mark as shown. Continue measuring, marking, and cutting as shown.

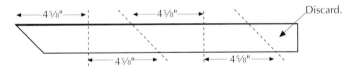

Discard.

4. Repeat steps 1–3 to cut the rest of the strips. Each 42"-long strip should yield 5 pairs of mirror-image trapezoids. Cut a total of 60 trapezoids.

5. Sew 1 red rectangle between each mirror-image pair of trapezoids. Press the seams toward the red print. Add a green print triangle to the short side of the unit as shown. Press the seams toward the triangle. Make 30 Triangle Tree units.

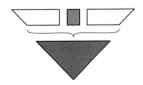 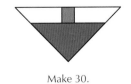

Make 30.

ASSEMBLING THE QUILT TOP & FINISHING

1. Arrange the Triangle Trees, Christmas Star, Chain, and Tree of Life blocks as shown. Sew the blocks and triangles together in diagonal rows. Press the seams toward the Chain blocks and Triangle Trees. Join the rows on the lower left and upper right sides of the Tree of Life block before sewing them to the block. Join the rest of the rows. Sew 2 Triangle Tree blocks together to make a large corner triangle. Add these to the quilt top last.

2. Cut 4 strips along the lengthwise grain of the red plaid, each 6" x 75". Measure across the center of the quilt top for border lengths, then trim the strips to fit. Sew border strips to the sides first, then to the top and bottom edges.

3. Layer the quilt top with backing and batting; baste.

4. Quilt as desired.

5. Bind the edges and label your quilt.

TROPICAL STAR

By Marge Hurst

This small wall hanging is one block with a pieced border. Directions and yardage requirements are provided for making one block with multiple background fabrics, using the leftovers for the borders. To make a larger quilt like "Starnet," simply make more blocks, and of course, purchase more fabric.

TEACHER'S QUILT: Tropical Sta[...]
by Marge Hurst, 1993
Pukerua Bay, New Zealand
27" x 27"

Meet the Teacher

*M*arge Hurst has been creating things with fabric and thread since she embroidered a pillowcase at age nine. She began doing patchwork while studying for the City and Guilds of London embroidery exam in the early 1980s. The patchwork assessment was the first section of the course, and Marge became hooked. She then carried on through the course, expanding her patchwork skills in addition to working on all the other embroidery topics.

After teaching a community-education class that featured a star theme, Marge began to play with one of the class exercises. While manipulating color, pattern, and geometric design, she noticed a lattice forming within the star framework. The result was "Starnet," which went on to win several awards, including Best of Show at the Sixth National Patchwork and Quilting Symposium in New Zealand. Since then, she has created several lattice designs and teaches a workshop called "Colour Through a Lattice." "Tropical Star" is just one block from "Starnet."

Christina Porter is one of Marge's loyal students. Christina's background is in fashion design, so working with fabric is second nature. Her piece was constructed with fabrics she had hand dyed only weeks before. When she discovered she didn't have enough fabric to make four complete blocks, a new shape was born.

Marge Hurst

Before buying materials, use the coloring diagram below to help you decide whether to use one background fabric or many. Photocopy the diagram and use colored pencils to play with color. Enlarge the coloring diagram if you prefer working with a larger design.

You can also place tracing paper directly over the diagram in the book or over a photocopy, and color the tracing paper. Marge prefers tracing paper because the black lines do not appear on the paper to interfere with the pattern, showing a more realistic rendition of the pattern.

When you have tried various color arrangements, rearranging lights, darks, and colors, purchase the required fabric, or go through your fabric stash to see what might be suitable. For the lattice, select a solid fabric or print that will contrast with the background. The background prints can contrast or blend with each other. Try hand-dyed fabric, bold contemporary or soft prints, or anything in between.

NOTE: Assign a number to each of the background fabrics and label the areas on the coloring diagram accordingly. When cutting and sewing the strip units, double-check the position of the fabrics with the coloring diagram. If you prefer to use only two fabrics, cut all background strips from the same fabric.

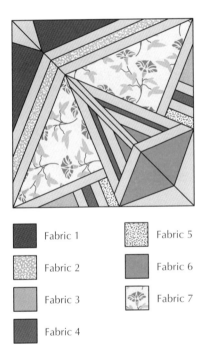

Fabric 1	Fabric 5
Fabric 2	Fabric 6
Fabric 3	Fabric 7
Fabric 4	

Finished Quilt Size: 27" x 27"

MATERIALS: *44"-wide fabric*

¾ yd. for lattice and inner border; choose a solid or print that contrasts with the background fabrics

⅛ yd. each of background fabrics 1, 2, 4, and 5*

¼ yd. each of background fabrics 3, 6, and 7*

1 yd. for backing

30" x 30" piece of thin batting

¼ yd. for binding

Or ⅞ yd. if you plan to use only one fabric for the background.

NOTE: Since you will need to cut 42"-long strips, do not purchase fat quarters.

CUTTING

Cut strips across the width of the fabric (crosswise grain).

Fabric	Strip Width	No. of Strips to Cut	Template	No. of Templates to Cut
Lattice	1"	15		
	1"	2 (for inner border)		
			E	4 & 4 reversed
			G	4 & 4 reversed
Background Strips				
Fabric #1	2¾"	1		
Fabric #2	1"	2		
Fabric #3	4¼"	1		
Fabric #4	1"	1		
	¾"	2		
Fabric #5	1"	1		
Fabric #6	1¼"	1	F	8
Fabric #7			C	8

MAKING TEMPLATES

1. Trace the templates on pages 75–76 onto template plastic or heavy card stock. Trace the guidelines on the front and back of the templates. Do not add seam allowances.
2. Cut out each template exactly on the traced line. If you make cardboard templates at least ⅛" thick, you can run the rotary cutter along the edge of the templates to cut the pieces. Otherwise, place a ruler on top of the templates and cut along the edge of the ruler. Be sure to label each template.

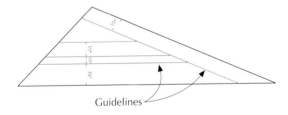

Guidelines

NOTE: Do not photocopy the templates. Photocopying will distort the lines, resulting in inaccuracies when you assemble the quilt.

Assembling the Center Block

Use an accurate ¼"-wide seam allowance.

1. Assemble 1 of each of the following strip units as shown. Press all seams open.

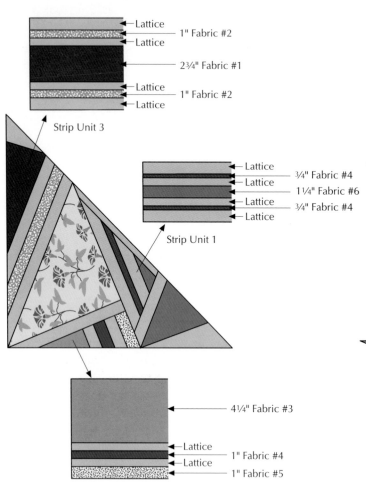

Strip Unit 3

Strip Unit 1

Strip Unit 2

— Lattice
— 1" Fabric #2
— Lattice
— 2¾" Fabric #1
— Lattice
— 1" Fabric #2
— Lattice

— Lattice
— ¾" Fabric #4
— Lattice
— 1¼" Fabric #6
— Lattice
— ¾" Fabric #4
— Lattice

— 4¼" Fabric #3
— Lattice
— 1" Fabric #4
— Lattice
— 1" Fabric #5

2. Cut 4 each of Template A2 and A2 reversed from strip unit 1 as shown. Align the template guidelines with the seams of the strip unit.

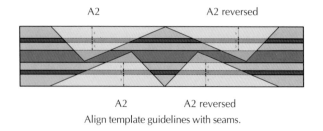

A2   A2 reversed

A2   A2 reversed
Align template guidelines with seams.

3. Add a lattice strip to 1 side each of the A2 and A2 reversed pieces, allowing a little extra length as shown. Press the seams open. Use Template A1 to trim the pieces; reverse the template to trim the reversed pieces.

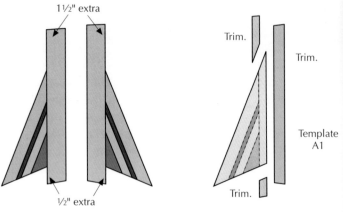

1½" extra

Trim.

Trim.

Template A1

½" extra

Trim.

4. Add a lattice strip to each short side of the A2 and A2 reversed pieces, allowing a little extra length as shown. Press the seams open. Use Template A to trim the pieces; reverse the template to trim the reversed pieces.

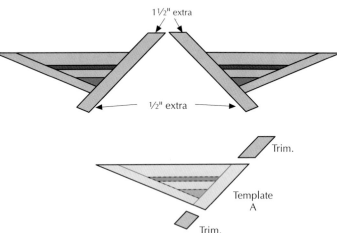

1½" extra

½" extra

Trim.

Template A

Trim.

5. Cut 4 each of Template B1 and B1 reversed from strip unit 2. Align the template guidelines with the seams of the strip unit.

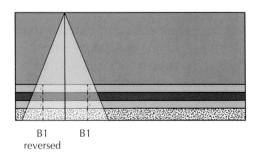

B1   B1
reversed

6. Add a lattice strip to one side each of the B1 and B1 reversed pieces, allowing a little extra length as shown. Press the seams open. Use Template B to trim the pieces; reverse the template to trim the reversed pieces.

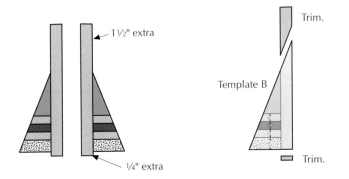

9. Assemble the units for Option 1 as shown. (Assembly for Option 2 is shown on page 74.) Match the raw edges and seams, and pin before stitching. Remember to press all the seams open.

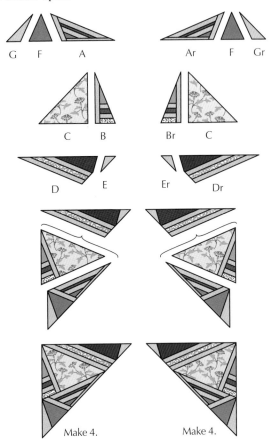

Make 4.   Make 4.

7. Cut 4 each of Template D and D reversed from strip unit 3 as shown. Align the template guidelines with the seams of the strip unit.

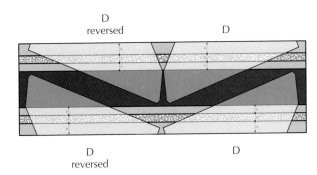

8. Before assembling the units, decide which arrangement you prefer. The difference between Option 1 and Option 2 is the placement of sections D and E in relation to the triangular section A/B/C/F/G.

Option 1

Option 2

10. Join 2 mirror-image sections to make a quarter block. Carefully pin the seams before stitching. Join the quarter blocks, then join the halves to complete the block.

NOTE: Assemble the units for Option 2 as shown.

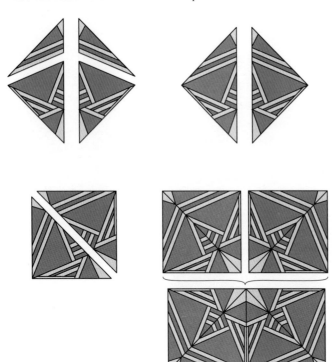

ADDING BORDERS

1. Add the 1"-wide inner border to the sides first, then to the top and bottom edges; or miter the corners.
2. For the outer border, cut segments from the remaining strip units and join them to create a border long enough for each side. If you cannot cut enough segments from the strip units to reach the required lengths, add more pieces cut from the other fabrics in the quilt. You could also use a 3"- or 4"-wide strip of a single fabric as a border. Experiment with your leftover fabric and create a border to fit your quilt.

FINISHING

1. Layer the quilt top with batting and backing; baste.
2. Quilt as desired.
3. Bind the edges and label your quilt.

"Starnet" on page 69 was primarily made in the same way as "Tropical Star." Because of the Colourwash effect across the quilt top, the strip units from which some of the template pieces were cut were shorter than those used in "Tropical Star." Marge made up a number of strip units with various fabric combinations, which were perhaps only long enough for two pairs of template pieces. Each of the cut pieces was then used in a different section of the quilt, rather than being arranged symmetrically. Colors were auditioned and strip units made as construction of the quilt progressed.

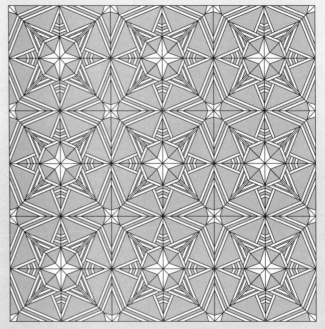

Starnet Quilt Diagram

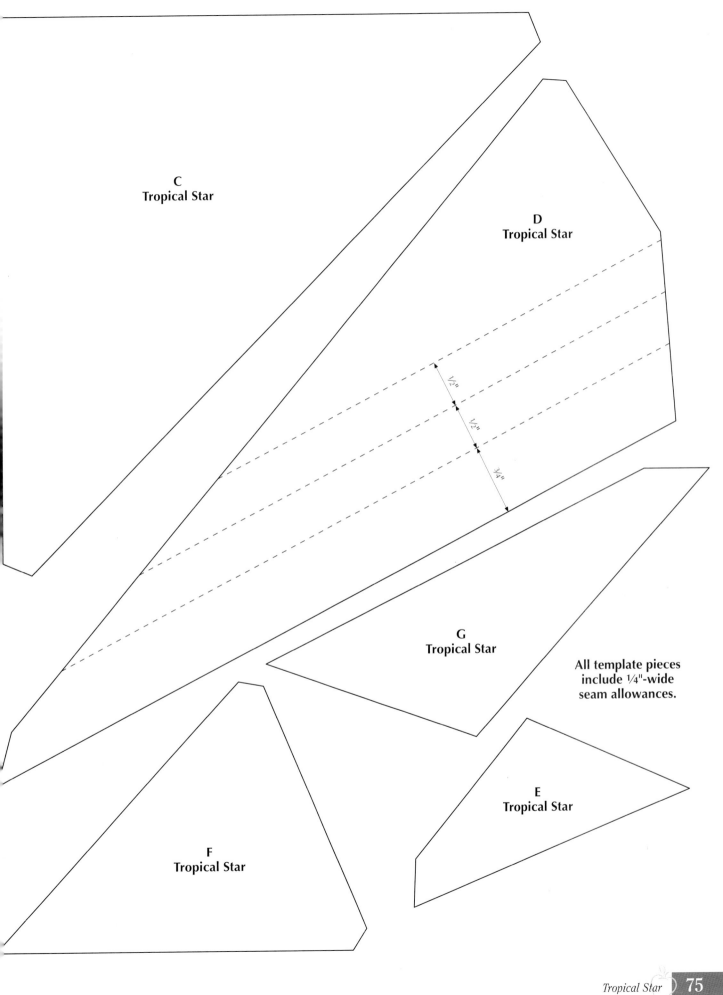

C
Tropical Star

D
Tropical Star

$1/2"$

$1/2"$

$3/4"$

G
Tropical Star

All template pieces
include $1/4"$-wide
seam allowances.

E
Tropical Star

F
Tropical Star

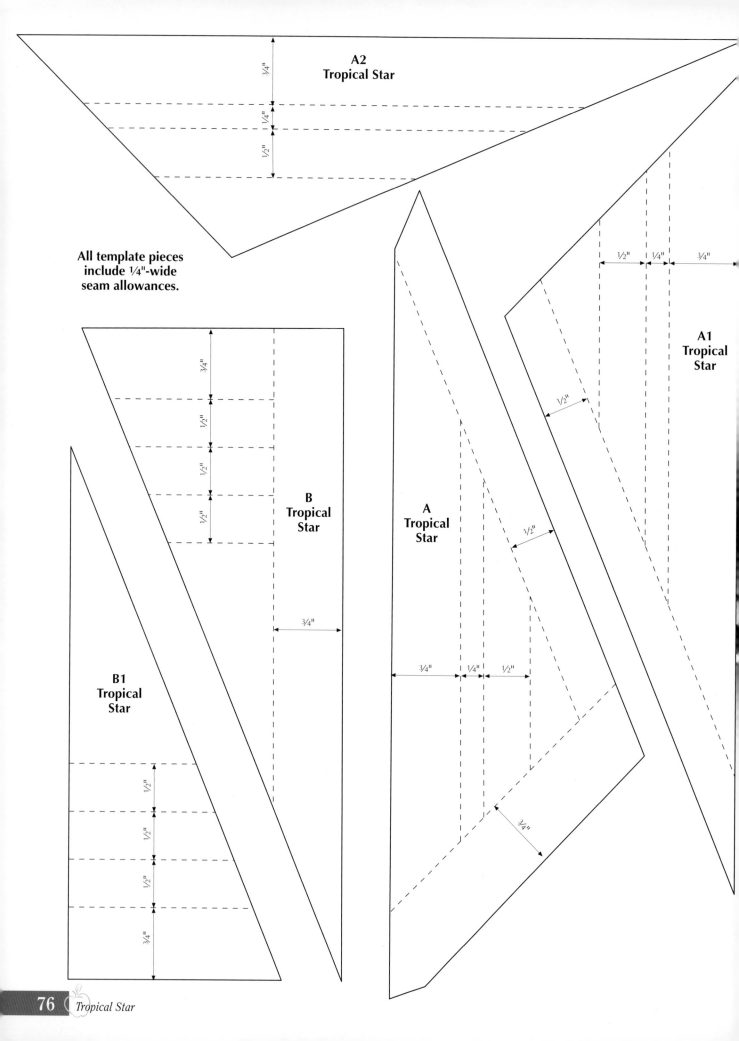

A2
Tropical Star

¾"

¼"

½"

All template pieces
include ¼"-wide
seam allowances.

A1
**Tropical
Star**

½" ¼" ¾"

½"

B
**Tropical
Star**

¾"

½"

½"

½"

A
**Tropical
Star**

½"

¾"

¾" ¼" ½"

B1
**Tropical
Star**

½"

½"

½"

¾"

MINIATURE UNCLE SAM QUILT

By Janet
Shurtleff

Janet & Gayle

Meet the Teacher

Janet Shurtleff learned to sew on her mother's old treadle sewing machine when she was very young. She bought her own sewing machine in high school and hasn't stopped sewing since. Even though Janet made a quilt when she was 14 years old, she didn't really start quilting until 1983, when she made her first wall quilt. It was a Dresden Plate quilt with a pieced, scalloped border. From that point on Janet channeled all her sewing efforts into quilts.

Janet is active in several quilt guilds, including the Utah Quilt Guild, and has served as president of the Ogden Quilt Guild. When asked to teach at the Utah Quilt Guild Annual Meeting, Janet designed the "Miniature Uncle Sam Quilt." The class was an instant success, and she has been teaching it ever since.

A collection of doll beds inspired Janet to make miniature quilts. Working with miniatures allows her to make a lot of patterns using many techniques. Because some of the pieces are quite small, she uses foundation paper-piecing methods to make the blocks.

Gayle Burton made her first quilt 20 years ago when she was just out of high school. Although she continued sewing for her family and home, she didn't start quilting again until 1993, when she joined a couple of local quilt guilds and became excited by new techniques and new friends. Gayle enjoys making seasonal quilts to decorate her home for the holidays, and scrap quilts are her favorites.

TEACHER'S QUILT:
Miniature Uncle
Sam Quilt
by Janet Shurtleff,
1995, Ogden, Utah,
13" x 11¼".

STUDENT'S QUILT:
Miniature Uncle Sam Quilt
by Gayle Burton, 1995,
Clinton, Utah,
13" x 12¼".

Finished Quilt Size: 13" x 11¼"

MATERIALS: *44"-wide fabric*

¼ yd. background for Uncle Sam block
⅛ yd. stripe for Uncle Sam's hat and pants
⅛ yd. each of assorted reds, blues, creams, tans, and greens
    for blocks
⅛ yd. for border
½ yd. for backing
⅛ yd. for binding
17" x 15" piece of thin batting
Embroidery floss for hearts and hand
2 small black beads for Uncle Sam's eyes
3 medium beads for vest buttons
Fuzzy yarn for Uncle Sam's beard
5 medium black snaps for watermelon seeds
Button for Square within a Square block

CUTTING

Cut pieces for the blocks as called for in the step-by-step directions.

From the border fabric, cut:

1 strip, 1½" x 10½", for top border*
2 strips, each 1½" x 11¼", for side borders*

From the binding fabric, cut:

2 strips, each 1¾" x 42"

*Janet's quilt does not have a bottom border. For 4 borders, as in Gayle's quilt, cut 2 strips, each 1½" x 11", for top and bottom borders, and 2 strips, each 1½" x 12¼", for side borders.

FOUNDATION PIECING

Foundation paper piecing is an easy method for piecing accurate blocks. A block design is transferred onto paper, fabric pieces are placed on the unmarked side of the paper, and seams are stitched on the marked side. Fabric pieces are added and sewn in numerical order. Generally, the paper is removed after the quilt top is assembled. To reduce bulk, Janet prefers to remove some of the paper from the center of the blocks as she works. The paper should not be removed from outer edges of the block until the blocks are joined. The finished block is the reverse of the drawn block design. Use the Square within a Square block as an example, following the same simple steps for foundation piecing each block.

Square within a Square Block

Finished Block Size: 3" x 3"

1. Trace the foundation block designs on pages 82–85 onto tracing paper, or make a photocopy of the patterns. Trim the blocks, allowing at least ½" outside the outer lines of each block.

   NOTE: Use the same photocopy machine for all the foundations to ensure that the blocks will fit together accurately.

2. Piece each block in numerical order. Cut fabric for piece 1 at least ½" larger all around than the finished size. Place piece 1 on the unmarked side of the paper, with the wrong side of the fabric toward the paper. Hold the paper up to a light source to make sure the fabric extends at least ¼" beyond the edges of piece 1.

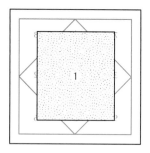

3. Cut fabric for piece 2, allowing at least ½" all around. Place piece 2 on top of piece 1, right sides together.

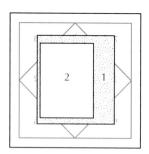

NOTE: A cut piece does not need to exactly match the desired shape. Often a square or a rectangle can be used, but it must be large enough to cover the desired piece plus seam allowances. It's better to be generous when cutting your pieces. You can always trim the excess, but you can't add on if a piece is too short.

4. Carefully turn the paper over so the marked side of the block is on top. If necessary, pin to hold the pieces in place. Stitch on the line between pieces 1 and 2, using a very short stitch (14 to 16 stitches per inch). Stitch just beyond the beginning and end at the line. Do not backstitch.

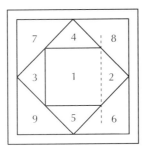

5. Turn back to the fabric side of the block. If necessary, trim the seam allowance to ¼". Flip piece 2 open and press.

6. Cut fabric for piece 3, allowing at least ½" all around. Place piece 3 in position, right sides together.

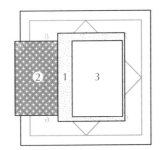

7. Carefully turn the paper over so the marked side of the block is on top. Stitch on the line between piece 3 and piece 1.

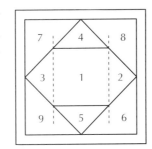

8. Turn back to the fabric side of the block. Trim the seam allowance to ¼" if necessary. Flip piece 3 open and press.
9. Continue cutting and adding pieces in the same manner until all the pieces for the block have been added.
10. Using a rotary cutter and ruler, trim ¼" beyond the outer line of the block foundation to allow for seam allowances.

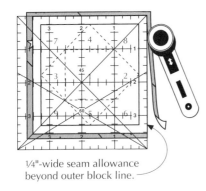

¼"-wide seam allowance beyond outer block line.

11. If desired, sew a decorative button in the middle of the center square.

Uncle Sam Block

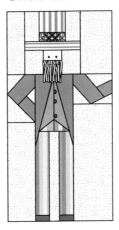

Finished Block Size: 4½" x 8¾"

The Uncle Sam block is made of several foundation-pieced sections, as well as several individual pieces. Treat the individual pieces as if they were foundation pieced. Trace the individual shapes onto paper, including the ¼"-wide seam allowance all around. Cut fabrics to cover the paper, plus a little extra all the way around. Baste the fabric to the paper and trim the edge to ¼" beyond the outer lines of the piece. Referring to the diagram below, follow the sequence to complete the Uncle Sam block.

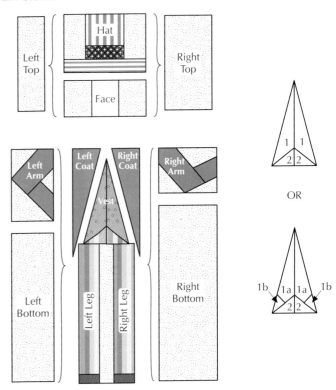

1. Foundation piece the hat, then the face. Sew the hat to the face. Add the left top and right top background pieces to the hat/face.
2. Foundation piece the left and right arms. Sew the left bottom background to the left arm. Sew the right bottom background to the right arm.

3. Foundation piece the left and right legs. Sew the background piece between the legs.
4. Foundation piece the left and right vests, treating 1a and 1b as a single piece. For a pointed vest front, construct 1a and 1b as separate pieces before adding piece 2. Use the same fabric for pieces 1b and 2 (these pieces are part of the pants).
5. Sew the left and right vest together. Sew the vest to the top of the pants, centering the seam in the middle of the background piece. Add the left and right coat pieces to the vest/pants.
6. Sew the left and right arm sections to the coat/vest/pants. Sew the hat/face to the top of the body.
7. Hand stitch 2 small beads to the face for eyes, or make French knots. Hand stitch 3 medium beads to the front of the vest, or make French knots.
8. Wrap the yarn around a 1¾" x 1½" piece of cardboard to desired thickness for the beard. Slide the yarn off the cardboard and carefully place the loops on a piece of paper. Make 3 or 4 rows of stitching through the yarn and paper, ¼" from 1 end of the looped yarn. Carefully remove the paper and cut through the loops at both ends. Trim to the desired length. Hand stitch the mustache/beard on the face just below the eyes.

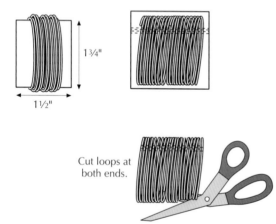

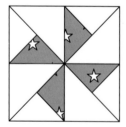

Cut loops at both ends.

Pinwheel Block

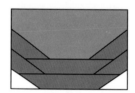

Finished Block Size: 3" x 3"

1. Foundation piece 2 half blocks.

2. Sew the halves together, matching the center seams.

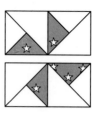

3. Trim the outside edge of the block, leaving a ¼"-wide seam allowance.

Sailboat Block

Finished Block Size: 3" x 3"

1. Foundation piece the block. Stripes cut on the diagonal work well for the sail pieces. You can use 1, 2, or 3 pieces for the boat hull (pieces 5a, 5b, and 5c).
2. Trim the outside edge of the block, leaving a ¼"-wide seam allowance.

Watermelon Block

Finished Block Size: 3" x 2"

1. Foundation piece the block.
2. Trim the outside edge of the block, leaving a ¼"-wide seam allowance.
3. Separate the black snaps and use the backs for the watermelon seeds. Hand stitch the snaps in place.

Flag Block

Finished Block Size: 3" x 3¾"

1. Foundation piece the flag portion of the block, pieces 1–8.
2. Cut a piece of background fabric, 2½" x 3¼".
3. Cut 1 big heart (Template 1) and 2 small hearts (Template 2). Appliqué the hearts to the background piece, or fuse using paper-backed fusible web and a buttonhole stitch (see below right) to finish the raw edges.
4. Foundation piece the heart section to the flag section. Add the flagpole (piece 10) to the left side.

5. Trim the outside edge of the block, leaving a ¼"-wide seam allowance.

Heart in Hand Block

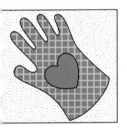

Finished Block Size: 3" x 2¾"

1. Cut a piece of background fabric, 3½" x 3¼".
2. Cut 1 hand (Template 3) and 1 heart (Template 4).
3. Appliqué the hand to the background piece, or fuse and use a buttonhole stitch to finish the raw edges. Repeat with the heart.

Bottom Border

Starting at one end, foundation piece the bottom border. Alternate reds, blues, greens, and creams for a scrappy look.

ASSEMBLING THE QUILT TOP & FINISHING

1. Arrange and sew the blocks and bottom border together as shown below.
2. Add the 1½" x 11" border strip to the top of the quilt.
3. Add the 1½" x 11¼" border strips to the sides.
4. Remove the paper from the blocks.

5. Layer the quilt top with batting and backing; baste.
6. Quilt as desired.
7. Bind the edges and label your quilt.

Buttonhole Stitch

Using 2 strands of embroidery floss, bring the needle up at point A through the background. Insert the needle at B and come up at C, just off the edge and over the thread. To continue, insert the needle at the next point B, keeping the stitches an even distance apart and an even distance into the motifs.

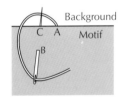

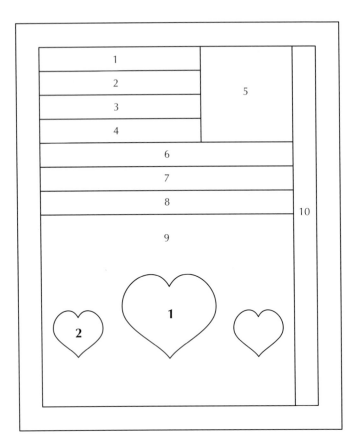

Flag Block

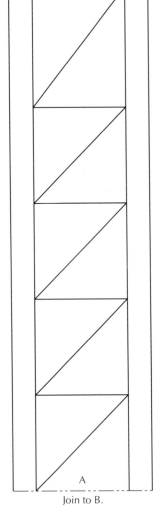

Join to A.

B

A

Join to B.

Bottom Border

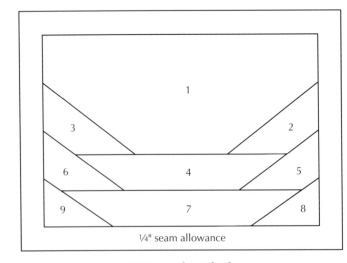

¼" seam allowance

Watermelon Block

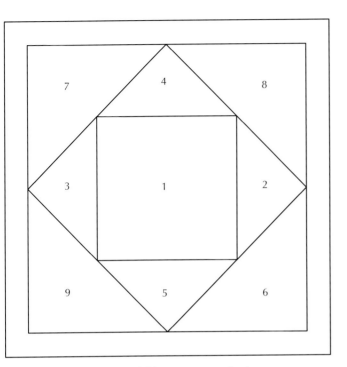

Square within a Square Block

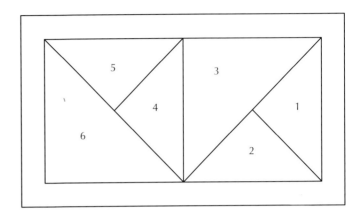

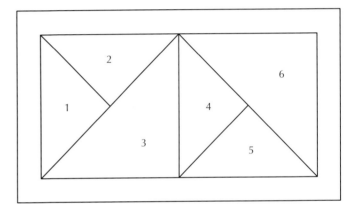

Pinwheel Block

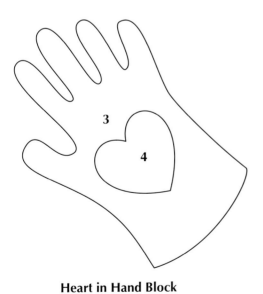

Heart in Hand Block

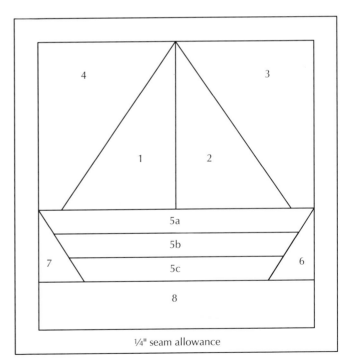

¼" seam allowance

Sailboat Block

Uncle Sam Hat and Face Section

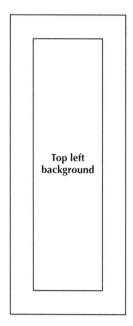

Top left background

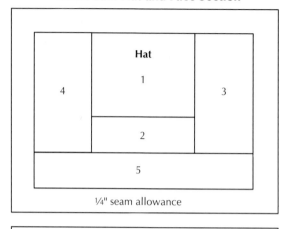

Hat

4

1

3

2

5

¼" seam allowance

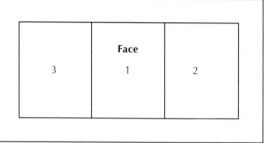

Face

3

1

2

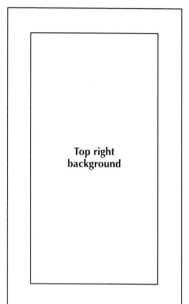

Top right background

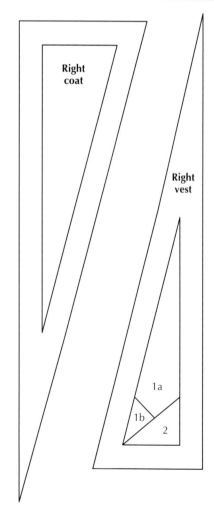

Right coat

Right vest

1a

1b

2

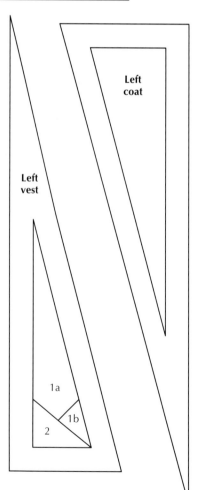

Left coat

Left vest

1a

1b

2

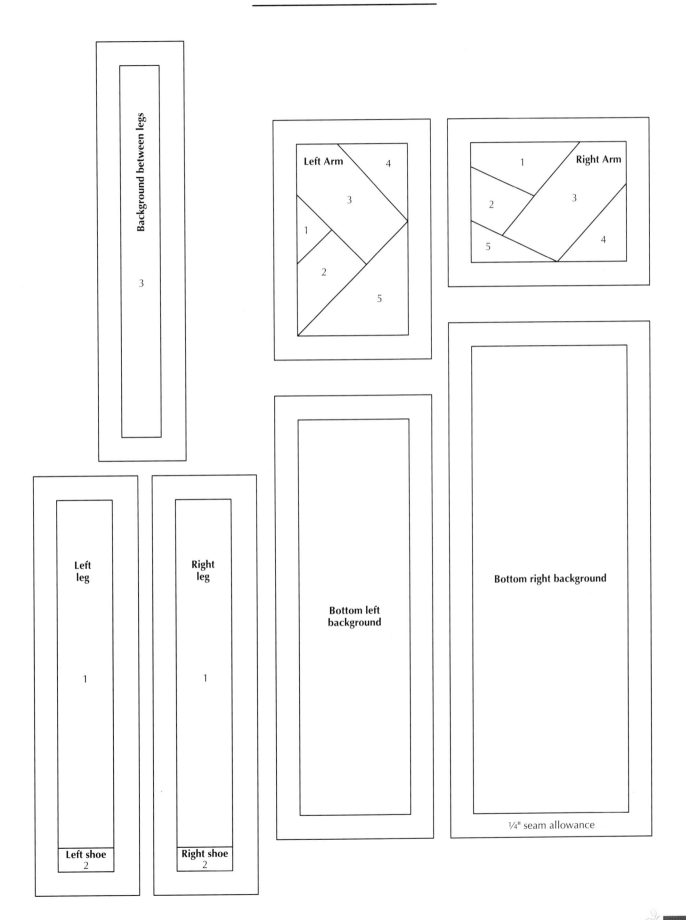

REACH FOR THE STARS

By Lynn Crawford

Kay & Lynn

Meet the Teacher

*L*ynn Crawford earned a
Bachelor of Arts in Industrial
Education in 1979; however, she
quickly realized teaching high
school students was not the
career for her and found work in
the aerospace field. That still did
not provide a creative outlet, but
when her stepmother introduced
her to quilting in 1983, Lynn
was hooked—big time!

Lynn started with a sampler
class, all done by hand. From
there she moved quickly to the
sewing machine and, in 1987,
taught her first quilting class.
Finally, she was able to put her
teaching education to use. She
has taught in numerous quilt
shops and guilds in California
and Nevada.

Lynn and her husband, Dale,
live the small town of
Wrightwood, California. There
she concentrates on her quilting
and the local Pine Needles Quilt
Guild. She teaches classes in her
log-cabin home and is also a
partner in The Traveling
Quilters, a tour service for
quilting enthusiasts.

"Reach for the Stars" was designed for
a beginners class. Her success with the
striped mitered borders is only one
example of what beginners can achieve
with proper instruction.

Kay Denny is a perfect example.
"Reach for the Stars" was her first quilting
class—and she even claims to hate
sewing! Kay's primary love is basket
weaving, but since baskets and quilts are
such naturals together, she decided to do
both.

TEACHER'S QUILT:
Reach for the Stars *by
Lynn Crawford, 1995,
Wrightwood, California,
44" x 44".*

STUDENT'S QUILT:
Reach for the Stars
*by Kay Denny, 1995,
Wrightwood, California,
44" x 44".*

Finished Quilt Size: 44" x 44"

MATERIALS: 44"-wide fabric

Choose a large-scale floral or paisley to use in the outer border and a few of the stars. Then select two color families to coordinate with your large-scale print, such as blue and yellow or red and green. The two coordinating colors are used to create the stars.

2 yds. for background
½ yd. large-scale blue-and-yellow floral print
¼ yd. *each* of 4 assorted blue prints
¼ yd. *each* of 4 assorted yellow prints
½ yd. for binding
3 yds. for backing*
52" x 52" piece of batting

Or purchase 1½ yds of backing and add pieces of leftover fabric to make a backing.

EIGHT-POINTED STAR BLOCK

Finished Block Size: 12" x 12"

Follow the directions below to make 3 blue stars. Then repeat the steps to make 3 yellow stars using 2 yellow prints.

From each of 2 blue prints, cut:

2 strips, each 3" x 42". Cut the end of the strips at a 45° angle as shown. To cut diamonds, place a ruler's 3" mark on the angled edge of the strip and cut along the right-hand edge of the ruler. Cut 12 diamonds from each strip for pieces A1 and A2, for a total of 24 diamonds.

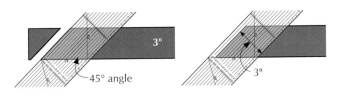

Cut 12 from each blue strip.

From the background fabric, cut:

12 squares, each 4" x 4", for piece B
3 squares, each 6¼" x 6¼"; cut the squares twice diagonally to yield 12 quarter-square triangles for piece C

1. On each piece mark dots at the ¼" intersections as shown.

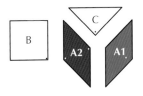

Tip Make plastic templates of each piece and punch a small hole at the seam intersections. Lay the plastic template on the fabric piece and mark the dots through the holes.

2. Sew pieces A1, A2, and C together in the order shown, stitching from the dots to the outer edges. Press the seams for piece C toward pieces A1 and A2. Press the seam between pieces A1 and A2 open. Make a total of 12 A1/A2/C units.

Tip Match the thread color to the dark fabric. Stitches tend to show on diamonds when light thread is used with dark fabrics.

3. Sew piece B to a unit made in step 2. Stitch from the dot to the outer edge. Press the seam toward piece A2. Make a total of 4 A/B/C units.

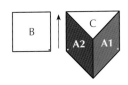

4. Sew the A/B/C units together in pairs. Stitch from the dots to the outer edges.

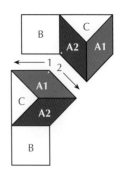

5. Join the 2 halves. Stitch from the outer edges to the dots. Sew the center seam last, stitching from dot to dot. Press the center seam open. Make a total of 6 Eight-Pointed Star blocks, 3 yellow and 3 blue.

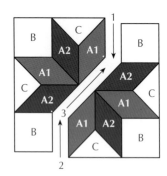

OHIO STAR BLOCKS

Finished Block Size: 9" x 9"

From the background fabric, cut:

12 squares, each 3½" x 3½"
3 squares, each 4¼" x 4¼"; cut the squares twice diagonally to yield 12 quarter-square triangles

From the blue-and-yellow floral, cut:

3 squares, each 3½" x 3½"

From 1 blue print, cut:

6 squares, each 4¼" x 4¼"; cut the squares twice diagonally to yield 24 quarter-square triangles

From 1 yellow print, cut:

3 squares, each 4¼" x 4¼"; cut the squares twice diagonally to yield 12 quarter square triangles

1. Join 2 blue triangles, 1 background triangle, and 1 yellow triangle as shown to make 1 star-point unit. Make a total of 12 star-point units.

Make 12.

2. Arrange 4 star-point units, 4 background squares, and 1 floral square as shown. Sew the units together in horizontal rows. Press the seams in opposite directions from row to row. Join the rows to complete 1 Ohio Star block. Make 3 blocks.

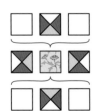

Make 3.

VARIABLE STAR BLOCKS

Finished Block Size: 3" x 3"

Cutting and piecing directions are for making 1 star. Using the remainder of the fabrics, make 2 or 3 stars from each yellow and blue print for a total of 22 stars.

From the background fabric, cut:

4 squares, each 1¼" x 1¼"
4 rectangles, each 1¼" x 2"

From 1 yellow or blue print, cut:

1 square, 2" x 2"
8 squares, each 1¼" x 1¼"

1. Draw a diagonal line from corner to corner on the wrong side of each 1¼" yellow (or blue) square. Place a marked square on one end of the background rectangle as shown. Sew on the drawn line. Trim the seam to ¼". Press the seam toward the star point. Repeat with another square at the opposite end of the rectangle. Make a total of 4 star-point units.

Stitch.   Trim.   Press.

Stitch.   Trim.   Press.
Make 4 for each block.

2. Arrange 4 star-point units, 4 background squares, and 1 yellow (or blue) square as shown. Sew the units in horizontal rows. Press the seams in opposite directions from row to row. Join the rows to complete 1 Variable Star block. Make a total of 22 blocks.

Make 22.

𝒜SSEMBLING THE QUILT TOP & FINISHING

From the background fabric, cut:

5 rectangles, each 3½" x 6½", for lattice
5 rectangles, each 3½" x 9½", for lattice
8 strips, each 1¼" x 42", for inner and outer borders

From the blue-and-yellow floral, cut:

4 strips, each 2" x 42", for middle border

1. Assemble the stars and lattice strips as shown to make 4 units. Join the units.

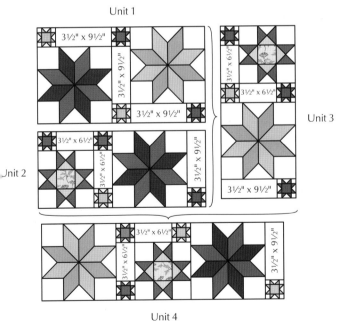

Unit 1

Unit 2

Unit 3

Unit 4

2. Sew 1¼"-wide background strips to each long edge of the 2"-wide floral strips. Press seams toward the floral strip.
3. Sew 1 Variable Star block to the left end of 2 pieced strips to make side borders. Sew 2 Variable Star blocks to the left end of the 2 remaining pieced strips to make the top and bottom borders

Side Borders
Make 2.

Top and Bottom Borders
Make 2.

4. Sew the border strips to the sides first, then add the top and bottom border strips. Stitch the ends without the stars to within ¼" of the quilt top edge. Miter the corners.

Stop stitching ¼" from edge.

Stop stitching ¼" from edge.

5. Layer the quilt top with batting and backing; baste.
6. Quilt as desired.
7. Bind the edges and label your quilt.

MINIATURE FOLK-ART QUILT

By Angela Krotowski

TEACHER'S QUILT: Miniature Folk Art Quilt *by Angela Krotowski, 1995, Aurora, Ontario, Canada, 26" x 26".*

Meet the Teacher

A self-taught quilter, Angela Krotowski, has been teaching quiltmaking since 1974. She teaches adult-education classes in her studio and for quilt guilds and quilt shops. She has also judged quilt-guild challenges and fairs.

Several of Angela's quilts have won awards and ribbons, but the most notable award was presented to her at the Canadian Quilters Association Conference in 1991. She received the Award of Excellence presented by That Patchwork Place for an appliquéd quilt titled "Floral Garden."

Angela readily shares her talents and skills with her community. She coordinated the design and execution of a historical quilt for her home-town, Aurora. The quilt depicts 20 historical houses in town and is displayed in the Municipal Building. Angela also finds time to act as the coordinator of Quilts from the Heart, a group of quilters who make quilts for a local woman's shelter. They meet at Angela's house once a month to sew quilts all day.

Although retired, Angela and her husband, John, run a small cottage industry from their home selling original patterns and quilting notions. They love to travel across Canada, participating in quilt trade shows and enjoying the sights.

A scrap of fabric given to Angela by a friend inspired the Miniature Folk-Art Quilt. That piece of fabric gave her the opportunity to combine creativity with her passion for appliqué.

Angela made both of the quilts shown, and a student, Cheryl Armstrong, quilted and beaded "Miniature Folk-Art Quilt #2."

TEACHER'S QUILT:
Miniature Folk-Art Quilt #2
by Angela Krotowski, 1995,
Aurora, Ontario, Canada,
26" x 26". (Embroidered and
beaded by Cheryl Armstrong)

Finished Quilt Size: 26" x 26"

MATERIALS: *44"-wide fabric*

Use lots of different prints in this quilt to make it more interesting. This project is a wonderful way to use up your fabric scraps.

1⅝ yds. for background, backing, and binding
Scraps, fat eighths, or fat quarters of assorted prints for appliqués
30" x 30" piece of low-loft batting
Embroidery floss for stems, block outlines, and borders
Freezer paper
Fabric-glue stick
¾"-long sequin pins
#10 (fine) or #12 (very fine) appliqué needles
Thread to match appliqué fabrics
Marking pencil: a fine lead (.5 mm) mechanical pencil for light fabric, a chalk marker for dark fabric

PREPARING THE BACKGROUND SQUARE

1. Cut a 28" x 28" square from the background fabric. This measurement allows for any shrinkage or fraying during the appliqué process. The square will later be trimmed to 26" x 26".
2. Following the diagram below, mark a 25½" square on the background fabric. Mark the center of each side and join these marks to make an 18" square set on point within the 25½" square. Mark 6" squares and 2"-wide sashing within the square.

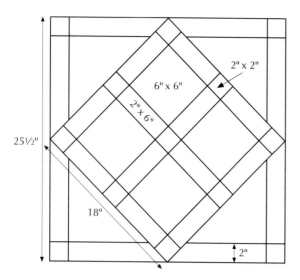

3. Using 6 strands of floss, embroider all marked lines with a backstitch (see page 94). Use a color that contrasts with your background.
4. Using the appliqué placement guides on the pullout pattern, mark the placement lines for the appliqué. Center each portion of the background fabric on top of the appropriate appliqué design and use a fine-point pencil to lightly trace just inside the design lines. If you are using a dark background fabric, mark only small sections at a time because chalk markers rub off easily.

MAKING FREEZER-PAPER TEMPLATES

Freezer-paper templates produce perfectly shaped appliqués because the paper sticks to the fabric and controls the shape. Accordion-fold the freezer paper and staple it to cut several of the same shape at one time.

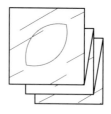

1. Place the freezer paper on the patterns, plastic side down. Trace each appliqué design with a sharp pencil.
2. Cut out the freezer-paper shapes on the pencil line. Do not add seam allowances.

PREPARING APPLIQUÉ PIECES

1. Iron the freezer-paper shape to the wrong side of the appliqué fabric, using a dry, hot iron.
2. Cut out the fabric shape, adding a ³⁄₁₆"-wide seam allowance.
3. Lay the pieces on a washable surface, paper side up. Using a toothpick, apply a small amount of glue from a glue stick to the seam allowance. Fold the seam allowance snugly over the freezer paper to form the appliqué shape; do not turn edges that will lie flat under other appliqué pieces. Clip curves and trim points as you work.

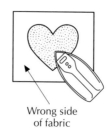

Wrong side
of fabric

4. Study the pattern and see which pieces are appliquéd first–always work from the background to the foreground.
5. Using the ¾"-long sequin pins, pin the appliqué shapes to the background fabric.

Appliquéing the Designs

1. Thread a needle with 12" of thread that matches your appliqué piece; knot the thread.
2. Starting with the knot on the back, take a stitch so the needle slants up through the edge of the appliqué fold. Go back down into the background at same spot, travel along under the background fabric, and repeat the stitch about ⅛" away. Continue around the appliqué shape. Do not stitch portions of an appliqué piece that will be covered by other pieces. End the stitching on the back, inside the appliqué shape, by taking 3 small stitches, one on top of the other.

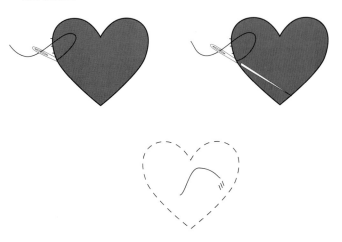

3. Embroider the stems with a stem stitch using 3 strands of embroidery floss. See page 94.

Making Bias Stems

Cut fabric into ½"-wide bias strips. Cut the length you need plus ½". Fold the strips in half lengthwise, wrong sides together, and press with a steam iron. Place the raw edges of the folded strip between the drawn lines. Using small running stitches, sew the strip to the background fabric, close to the raw edge. Sew a backstitch every few stitches to secure the stem. This line of stitching should cover one side of the stem line. Roll the folded edge over the seam allowance. Appliqué the fold to the background fabric, covering the other side of the stem line to create a smooth, thin stem.

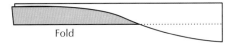

Fold

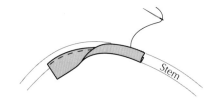

Stem

$\mathcal{M}$AKING CIRCLES

Method One

1. Draw a circle on the right side of the fabric. Cut out the circle ¼" outside the drawn line. Sew a small running stitch within the seam allowance.
2. Carefully pull the thread to form a circle. Flatten the circle and press with a steam iron.

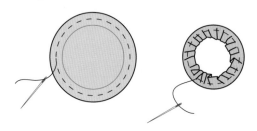

3. Pin the circle to the background fabric (gathered side down). Do not cut the thread. Use the thread to appliqué the circle, using smaller-than-usual stitches.

Method Two

1. Cut a template of heavy paper, exactly the size of the finished circle.
2. Using the paper template as a guide, cut a fabric circle, adding a ¼"-wide seam allowance around the edge of the template. Sew a small running stitch within the seam allowance, at least ⅛" from the edge.
3. Place the paper template in the center of the fabric circle. Pull the thread ends to gather the seam allowance around the paper. Steam press the circle, then let it rest a minute.

Paper template

4. Carefully peel back the fabric and remove the paper. Gently pull the basting threads to tighten the seam allowance and make it lie flat. Tie a knot.
5. Pin the circle to the background fabric and appliqué with smaller-than-usual stitches.

$\mathcal{F}$INISHING

1. After all the appliqué is complete, turn your work to the wrong side. Make a slit in the background fabric behind each appliqué piece, being careful not to cut into the appliqués.

2. Soak the quilt top in lukewarm water for 10 minutes. Using tweezers, carefully pull out the wet freezer paper and discard. Soak the quilt top again to remove the last trace of glue; the fabric should no longer feel slippery. Spread the quilt out flat on a towel, and when almost dry, press first on the wrong side and then lightly touch up on the right side.
3. Layer the quilt top with batting and backing; baste.
4. Quilt around each appliqué piece and along the embroidered lines.
5. Trim the quilt top to 26" square.
6. Bind the edges and label your quilt.

EMBROIDERY STITCHES

Backstitch

Bring the needle up through the fabric at point A. Insert the needle at B and come up at C. Pull the thread through. The distance between A and C should be the same as between A and B. Insert the needle at D (just next to the first point A) and come up at the next point A. Make sure each stitch touches the previous one, creating a smooth line.

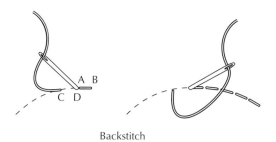

Backstitch

Stem Stitch

Bring the needle up through the fabric at point A. Insert the needle at B, about ¼" away, and come up again at C, halfway between A and B. Pull the thread through, holding the thread below the needle. To continue the stitch, insert the needle at D and come up again at B, the same place where the needle went into the fabric for the last stitch. Pull the thread through, holding the thread below the needle.

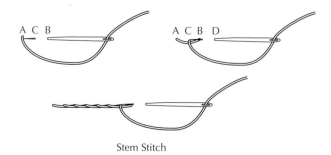

Stem Stitch

TWO-FABRIC WATERCOLOR

By Joanne Case

Karen & Joanne

TEACHER'S QUILT: ROSES *by Joanne Case, 1995, Sultan, Washington, 30" x 35".*

Joanne Case enjoys all forms of sewing and needlework, but quilting is at the top of her list. She considers herself a nontraditional quilter, although she loves traditional designs.

After making watercolor quilts using several-hundred fabrics, Joanne thought it would be a wonderful challenge to create a quilt using only two. Soon she was hooked on two-fabric watercolor quilts.

Joanne loves to share her quilting knowledge and has been an enthusiastic teacher for eight years. Her students often claim they aren't creative, and she tells them they're wrong. With a little encouragement and some fabric, Joanne's students are amazed to discover that they, too, can create unique designs.

Joanne and her husband, Ron, live in Sultan, Washington.

Karen Browne has been quilting for thirteen years. Her favorite quilts are traditional designs, so it took some gentle persuasion to get her to try a two-fabric watercolor quilt. However, since the persuader was not only the teacher, but also her mother, she could hardly refuse. "Bumbershoot" is Karen's first two-fabric watercolor quilt.

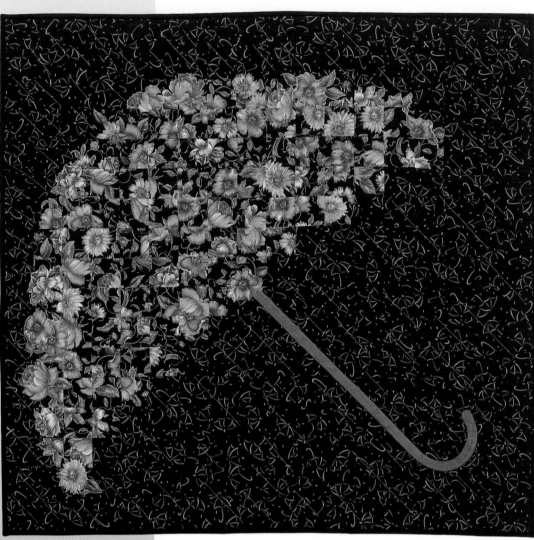

STUDENT'S QUILT
Bumbershoot
by Karen Browne, 1995
Sultan, Washington
36" x 36"

The instructions below will guide you in creating a bouquet similar to "Roses." Since fabric designs vary widely, the bouquet you create will not be identical—that's what makes it so exciting. Each quilt is unique, an original design.

A bouquet of flowers is only one possibility. You can produce anything you can imagine. You may even get help from the fabric itself. The inspiration for "Bumbershoot" came from the background fabric, which is printed with umbrellas. Try a heart, a basket of fruit, a wreath, trees, boats, a grape arbor, or even a landscape. Directions for making another of Joanne's two-fabric watercolor designs, a poinsettia wreath, can be found in *Quilted for Christmas, Book III.*

Finished Quilt Size: 30" x 35"

MATERIALS: 44"-wide fabric

Recommended fabrics: For the bouquet, choose a medium- to large-scale print with a scattered design and some background showing between the flowers. For the background, select a subtle print, solid, or tone-on-tone that closely matches the color of the floral print background.

1 yd. floral print for bouquet
1 yd. coordinating print for background
1 yd. for backing
⅓ yd. for binding
1 yd. low-loft batting
¼ yd. paper-backed fusible web
Iron-on or tear-away stabilizer for machine embroidery
Machine-embroidery hoop
Metallic and/or rayon thread for machine embroidery and quilting

CUTTING

Cut all strips across the fabric width (crosswise grain).

From the floral print, cut:
• to 8 strips, each 3" x 42"; crosscut into 3" x 3" squares*

From the coordinating print, cut:
• to 8 strips, each 3" x 42"; crosscut into 3" x 3" squares*

Save remaining fabric for cutting more strips and squares as needed.

CREATING THE DESIGN

Pin a piece of flannel or needlepunch batting on the wall to use as a design surface. Not only will your squares stay in place as you arrange them, you'll also be able to stand back and evaluate your design while you work.

1. Begin the layout by setting the quilt's boundaries. Place background fabric squares across the top, bottom, and sides to form the outline of the quilt as shown. "Roses" is 12 squares wide and 14 squares long.

   Next, add background squares as shown to reserve space for the vase. The vase is about 4 squares high and 2 squares wide, positioned at the bottom center of the quilt.

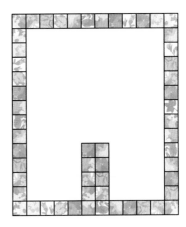

2. Sort the floral squares into 3 stacks:
   A: Squares with a heavy concentration of flowers and small amount of background

   B: Squares with about half flowers and leaves, and half background

   C: Squares with a lot of background and only a few flowers and leaves

3. Begin shaping the bouquet with squares from stack A. Start at the top of the vase and place them in a roughly circular shape as shown. Turn or move the squares around until colors blend from square to square and larger flower shapes emerge. Work toward blending the design and the color to eliminate abrupt changes from square to square. View your progress from a distance or through a reducing glass to locate squares that need attention.

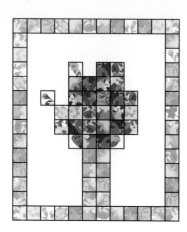

4. Select squares from stack B and place them around the perimeter of the bouquet. Blend the colors and shapes to suggest stems and flowers that are extensions of the ones in the center.

5. Add squares from stack C to the perimeter of the bouquet to "thin out" the flowers. Make some of the stems longer than others for a natural-looking bouquet.

6. Fill in the area surrounding the bouquet with background fabric.

Tip Try using the wrong side of your fabrics in some areas for more variety. Wrong sides will also produce subtle shading that softens the edges of the bouquet or suggests shadows. Using the wrong side of the fabric in the vase area may give the impression of water seen through crystal. Metallic thread will define the shape of the vase.

Assembling the Quilt Top

1. Join the squares in rows, being careful to keep them in the proper order. Press the seams in opposite directions from row to row.

2. Join the rows, carefully aligning the squares. Press the seams in one direction.

Softening the Edges

Put the quilt top on your design wall. Look for areas where the flowers and leaves end abruptly and for areas that need more flowers and leaves. "Fussy cut" partial flowers and leaves to soften the edges of the bouquet for a more natural look.

1. Look through the leftover squares and remaining fabric for just the right shapes. Apply paper-backed fusible web to the wrong side of the selected fabrics.

2. Carefully cut out the desired shapes and remove the paper backing. Position the shapes on the quilt top and iron in place following the manufacturer's directions.

Fussy cutting

3. Repeat this process as needed to enhance the composition. Add a few flowers to hang over the top of the vase. Add 1 or 2 flowers under the bouquet to represent blossoms lying on a table.

Painting with Thread

NOTE: If you are new to thread-painting, read through the following steps and practice on scrap fabric before working on your quilt. If necessary, adjust the machine tension so the bobbin thread does not pull to the top.

1. Trace the vase pattern on page 101 onto tracing paper. Position the paper on the quilt top and pin securely in place.

2. Set your machine stitch length at 12 to 14 stitches per inch. Stitch on the traced lines with thread that closely matches the background fabric. The stitched outline of the vase will act as a guide for your metallic-thread painting. Remove the tracing paper.

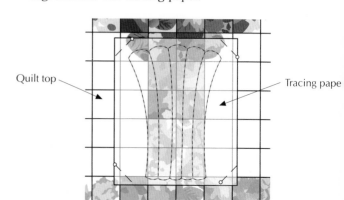

Quilt top

Tracing paper

3. Add iron-on or tear-away stabilizer to the back of the vase-area fabric.
4. Place as much of the vase area into a machine-embroidery hoop as possible. Stretch the fabric evenly and tightly to prevent puckering when stitching. Move the hoop as necessary to stitch the entire vase.
5. Install a darning foot on your machine and lower or cover the feed dogs for free-motion stitching.
6. Thread the machine with metallic thread on top. Replace the needle with one designed for metallic thread. For the bobbin, use regular sewing thread or special machine-embroidery bobbin thread.
7. Set the machine for a medium to wide zigzag stitch and to half-speed sewing (if your machine offers this feature). Stitch along the inside edges of the vertical lines that represent the outside edges of the vase. Stitch all other vertical lines on one side only.

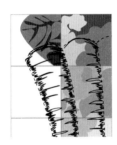

8. Maintain an even, moderately fast sewing speed and a light touch on the hoop, keeping your hands at the 3 o'clock and 9 o'clock positions. Use the needle as if it were a pencil shading the grooves of the vase. As you follow the lines upward or downward, move the quilt back and forth horizontally. Keep the horizontal movements slow and even. This movement can seem awkward at first, so practice ahead of time.
9. Vary the length of the lines for a more natural look. For best results, stitch the lines in two or three passes rather than trying to fill a line in just one pass.

SECURING THE FUSED PIECES

1. Thread the machine with clear nylon or decorative rayon thread. Change the machine setting to a straight stitch or narrow zigzag. (Continue to work in free-motion with the feed dogs dropped.)
2. Pin stabilizer under the fused pieces and place the fabric in an embroidery hoop.

3. Stitch over the raw edges of the fused pieces. This provides additional security so the edges will not lift away from the quilt.

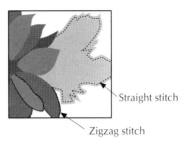

Straight stitch

Zigzag stitch

STEM ON THE TABLE

1. Trace the stem pattern on page 100 or draw your own with a removable fabric marker.
2. Change the machine setting to a medium-width zigzag. Use a variegated green thread to satin-stitch the stem.

Satin stitch

QUILTING THE BOUQUET

1. Layer the quilt top with batting and backing; baste with #1 safety pins.
2. Thread the top spool with a color that blends with the flowers; thread the bobbin with a color that matches the backing. Set the machine to straight stitching, leave the feed dogs down, and install the darning foot.
3. Using the free-motion sewing techniques described in "Painting with Thread," begin quilting at the center of the quilt and work out to the edges. Maintaining a continuous line of stitching, randomly outline and define the flowers and leaves, adding details as you go.

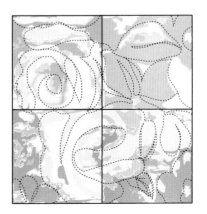

Keep the density of the quilting evenly distributed. If parts of the quilt are quilted too heavily, they will pucker and stiffen.

4. At the perimeter of the bouquet, add a few tendrils and free-form leaves. Either "draw" them free-hand with the needle or mark them ahead of time.

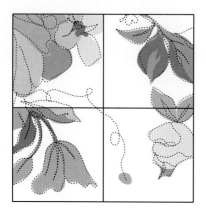

6. Quilt the vase following the original stitching lines.
7. Quilt around the flower and stem that lies on the table.

$\mathcal{F}$INISHING

1. Raise the feed dogs. Install an even-feed (walking) foot.
2. Set the stitch length slightly longer than normal and adjust the tension to normal.
3. Stitch in-the-ditch between the background squares both vertically and horizontally. Stop at the edges of the bouquet and secure the threads: backstitch, stitch in place, or leave threads long enough to tie off and bury between the layers of the quilt.
4. Add 2 more lines of evenly spaced stitching to one side of the ditch. Use the edge of the presser foot as a guide.

5. Bind the edges and label your quilt.

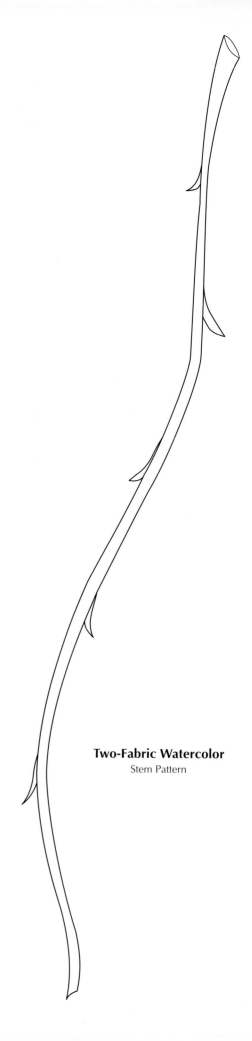

Two-Fabric Watercolor
Stem Pattern

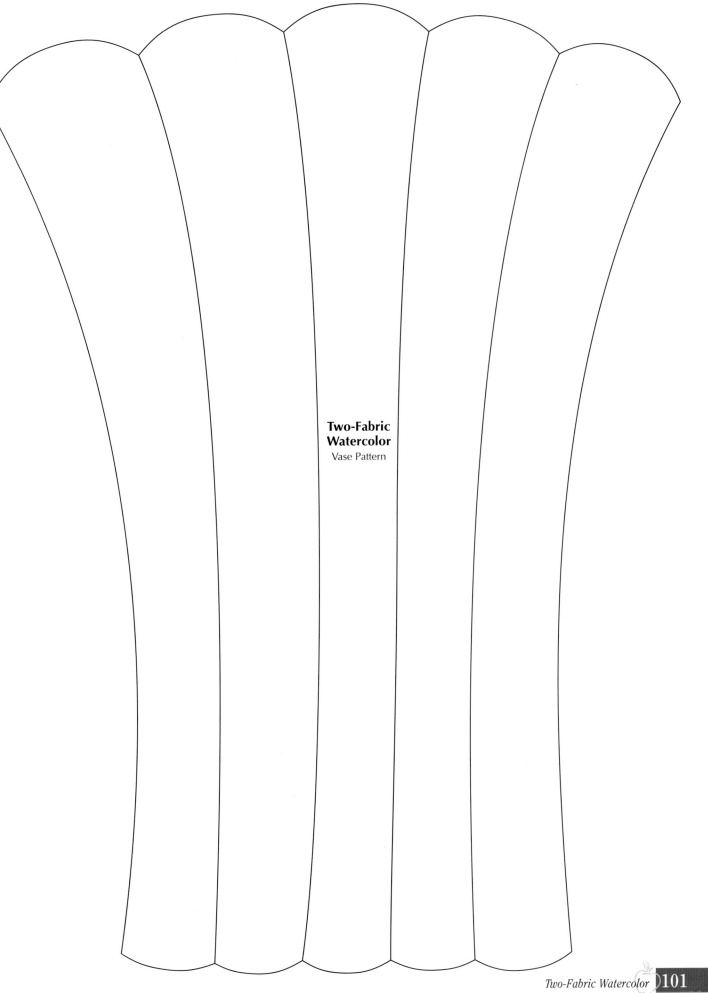

Two-Fabric Watercolor
Vase Pattern

COLORFIELDS

By Meiny Vermaas-van der Heide

Meet the Teacher

*B*orn in the Netherlands, Meiny Vermaas-van der Heide spent most of her life surrounded by flowers. After moving to the United States in 1985, she missed the everyday pleasure of bouquets in the house. Now Meiny's contemporary quilts have become her flowers, stirring the same feelings of love and friendship that Baltimore Album quilts inspired a century ago.

The "Colorfields in Geometric Abstraction" workshop started as Meiny's self-guided study of visual illusions within quilt surfaces. Based on a simple geometric design, Meiny's Fields of Color quilts are fabulous explorations of color, value, and visual texture.

Meiny sees her workshops as a creative-growth experience for all participants, including herself. Promoting self-esteem in a positive, encouraging way is one of her classroom priorities.

Trained as a teacher in home economics and health education, Meiny has been teaching quiltmaking and design since 1992. She has taught in Europe and the United States, including workshops at the International Quilt Festival in Houston and the New York Quilt Festival.

Design students and quiltmakers of all levels—such as beginner Anne Barry, who made "Owls Hide in My Garden"—feel very much at ease in Meiny's workshops, because she gives each participant individual attention, advice, and critiques.

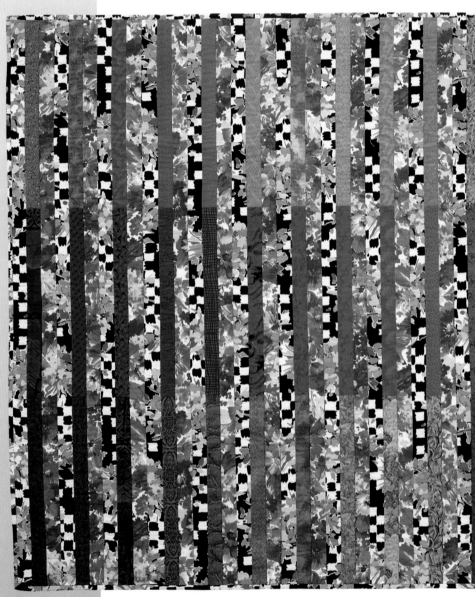

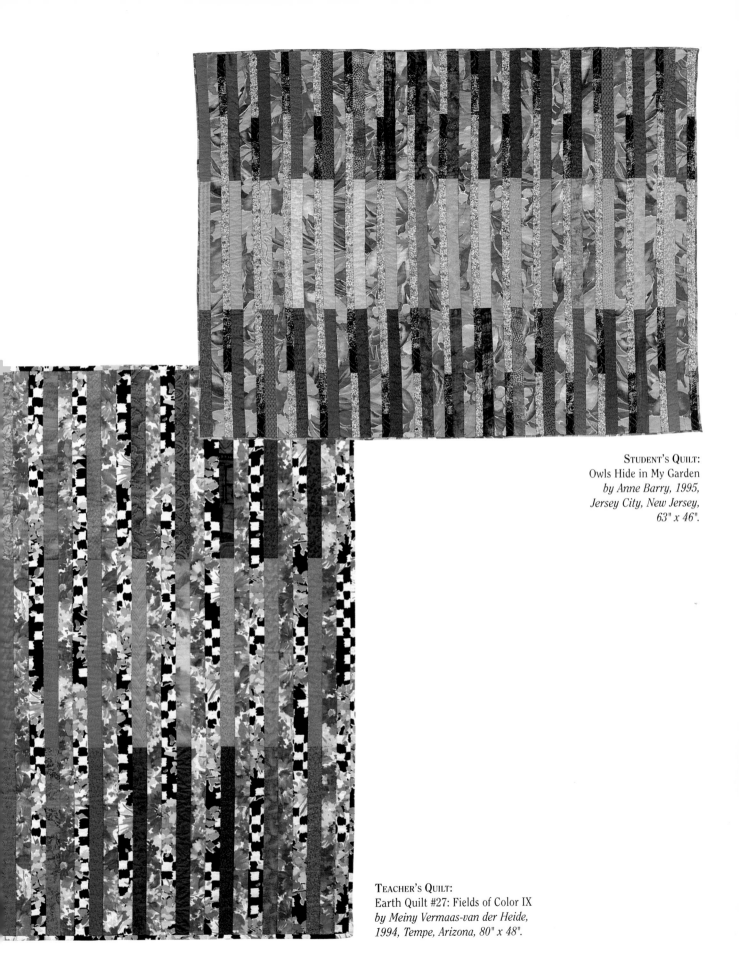

STUDENT'S QUILT:
Owls Hide in My Garden
by Anne Barry, 1995,
Jersey City, New Jersey,
63" x 46".

TEACHER'S QUILT:
Earth Quilt #27: Fields of Color IX
by Meiny Vermaas-van der Heide,
1994, Tempe, Arizona, 80" x 48".

103

Green-blue | Orange → Yellow-orange | Bridge fabric | Mustard | Aqua blue → Green-blue | Blue-purple

Purple-red | Bridge fabric | Red → Orange-red | Orange → Yellow-orange | Bridge fabric | Mustard

Blue-purple | Green-blue → Aqua blue | Monochromatic purple | Green-blue

Meiny's "Fields of Color" series is an exploration of foreground and background in design. The series is inspired by the fields of flowers that cover the Dutch landscape.

Three sets of vertical strips are used: two base fabrics and one pieced unit of three filler strips that make up horizontal color blocks. A multicolored base fabric represents flowers. A black-and-white base fabric represents shadows beneath the flowers and between the foliage. The pieced color blocks represent rows of color as seen from a distance. Refer to the photo of "Earth Quilt #27: Fields of Color IX" on the previous page and the illustration above to see how the color blocks change across the surface of the quilt.

The interplay of color, texture, and value—what Meiny refers to as "visual illusion"—produces a vibrant design. The color blocks bring out and intensify their complements in the multicolored base fabric, and the perceived color of the filler strips changes depending on the color of the adjacent base strips. There is something new to discover every time you look.

SELECTING FABRICS

Choose a large-scale black-and-white base fabric that has a varying pattern density. From a distance, it should look as though there are different values (light and medium or medium and dark). In "Earth Quilt #27: Fields of Color IX," Meiny used a geometric black-and-white base fabric with a regular pattern of floral bouquets. These bouquets create areas of texture-on-texture in the quilt. For "Owls Hide in My Garden," Anne Barry used three black-and-white base fabrics to create different values within the black-and-white strips.

For the multicolored base fabric, choose a large-scale floral print, making sure there is not a lot of solid white or black in the background. "Multicolored" means at least four color groups. "Large-scale" means that when you cut the fabric into 1¼"- to 2"-wide strips, the print pattern will be continued in the next strip.

The filler strips create the horizontal color blocks. Let the multicolored base fabric be your color guide for selecting the solid and solid-reading fabrics for the filler strips. These fabrics, placed in three horizontal rows, should create an undulating value gradation within the color blocks. You can use a variety of color schemes for each of the color blocks. Try a monochromatic scheme—tints, tones, and shades of one color, ranging from light to dark. Consider analogous colors—colors next to each other on the color wheel, such as red-orange, orange, and orange-yellow.

Consider the following ideas and variations for using filler strips in your design:

- In "Owls Hide in My Garden," the filler strips in the top and bottom row are pushed toward the dark values of the multicolored base fabric, while the middle row is pushed toward the lighter values. Sometimes Anne used the wrong side of the fabric to get the lighter value she needed for the filler strips.

- A graduated value run is a color transition through part of the color wheel, in one or more color blocks, that changes in value from dark to medium or medium to light. A gradated value run can also go from medium to light to medium again, then to dark. The transition of colors within and between the color blocks does not need to be smooth. Because the base strips interrupt the color blocks, your eye reads the gradation as smooth, even if it is not.
- Balance the visual weight of the color blocks in the quilt surface, either symmetrically or asymmetrically. A simple way to do this in the top and bottom row is to reverse the order of the filler strips: from left to right in the top row and from right to left in the bottom row.
- Try offsetting the color blocks. Not all color blocks should stop or start in the same vertical design-unit strip. Make the transition between the color blocks with light, medium, or dark fabric, or use a two-color bridge fabric of the same value as the filler strips on either side of it.
- The filler strips create a horizontal, undulating value gradation. When there is an abrupt transition between the color blocks, the undulating effect is stronger.

  Where the filler strips are relatively dark in value, they appear to be in the foreground, the black-and-white base fabric seems to be behind the filler strips, and the multicolored base fabric lower still. Where the filler strips are relatively light in value, the black-and-white base fabric appears to be in the foreground.
- The quilts on pages 102–103 have three horizontal rows of filler strips, but you can use 5, 7, or 9. Do not, however, use filler strips less than 6" long.
- Vary the width of the filler strips, but keep them the same within a single vertical strip.

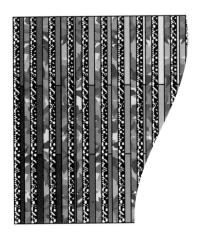

- Cut filler strips different lengths to create horizontal rows of varying sizes.

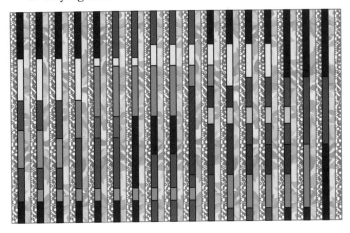

- The gradated value runs within and between the filler strips should have an interesting mix of visual textures. Do not place filler strips of similar visual texture directly next to or underneath each other. Sometimes switching the strips helps; at other times, moving the whole color block one or two places to the left or right might be the simple solution. Another option is to delete or add one or two strips. An exception to all this is hand-dyed gradations in solid colors only, because all the fabrics have the same visual texture, and this can be very effective.

For the color blocks, you need to choose fabrics in color groups that coordinate with your multicolored floral print. With regard to the question of how many filler strips to cut from each color group, think about the proportions of each color you want to use. If you are using complementary colors—colors opposite each other on the color wheel—there are guidelines for creating harmonious proportions. They are:

Purples : yellows	3 : 1
Blues : oranges	2 : 1
Reds : greens	1 : 1

The guidelines are not an exact science. Go by what feels right, and trust your intuition.

DESIGN VARIATIONS

- Use more than one black-and-white base fabric, either horizontally or vertically.
- Use more than one multicolored base fabric, either horizontally or vertically.
- Use a different multicolored floral fabric for the top and bottom row of the color blocks, thus creating integrated horizontal borders.

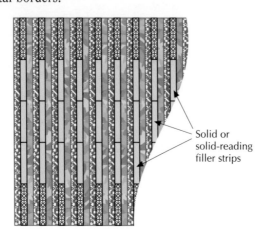

Solid or solid-reading filler strips

- Vary the width of the strips cut from one or both of the base fabrics. The visual illusions will change because of the greater density of visual texture.

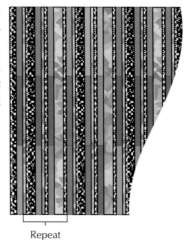

Repeat

- Use just one base fabric to create a checkerboard grid. The base fabric should have both large-scale multicolored areas and areas similar to a black-and-white base fabric.

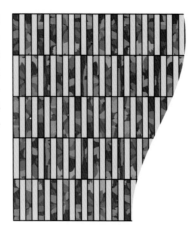

- Use Bargello-type strip piecing and crosscut the filler strips. Instead of horizontal bands, you will get irregularly shaped areas of color.

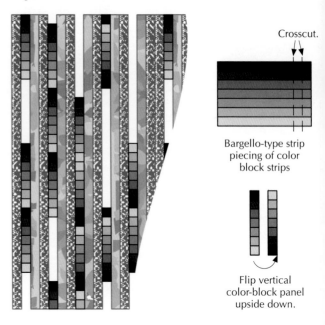

Crosscut.

Bargello-type strip piecing of color block strips

Flip vertical color-block panel upside down.

- Add yet another dimension to the quilt surface by inserting any number of 1"-wide vertical strips of black fabric. Only ½" of these strips will be visible when sewn.

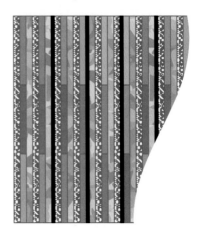

- Combine one or more of the above variations within one quilt for the ultimate design challenge.

Finished Quilt Size: 80" x 48"

Follow the directions below to make a quilt similar to Earth Quilt #27: Fields of Color IX." If you are intrigued by one of the variations above, adjust the directions accordingly to suit your design.

MATERIALS: 44"-wide fabric

1½ yds. black-and-white base fabric
1½ yds. multicolored floral base fabric
20 to 30 assorted fat eighths, fat quarters, or ½-yd. cuts of solids or solid-reading prints for filler strips. You will need a total of 60 strips; some duplicates are allowed.
5 yds. for backing and top and bottom hanging sleeves
⅝ yd. of one of the base fabrics for binding
54" x 96" piece of cotton batting for the design wall, which later can be used as batting for the quilt. Choose batting that is appropriate for the amount of quilting you plan to do later. A queen-size batting yields two 54" x 96" pieces.

DETERMINING THE STRIP WIDTH

The finished width of the base strips should be anywhere from ¾" to 1½". This means you can cut strips between 1¼" to 2" wide, which includes ¼"-wide seam allowances. To decide how wide to cut the strips, consider the following:

- If the two base fabrics have a similar amount of white, cut the strips the same width.
- If the black-and-white base fabric contains more white than the multicolored base fabric, cut the multicolored vertical strips wider than the black-and-white strips.

In "Earth Quilt #27: Fields of Color IX," all strips were cut 2" wide, despite the fact that white predominates in the black-and-white base fabric. If she'd used a narrower strip, Meiny would have lost the print's checkerboard in the ⅜"-wide seam allowance she prefers to use. (The directions for this quilt call for ¼"-wide seam allowances.)

Anne cut her strips 1½" wide from the black-and-white fabrics, 2" wide from the multicolored fabric, and 2" wide for the filler strips. Because Anne's initial choice for the black-and-white base fabric was too light, without enough black and contrast, it was not the best choice. She made it work, however, by combining it with two other black-and-white fabrics that clearly create multiple values from a distance.

CUTTING & POSITIONING STRIPS

Cut all strips from the lengthwise grain of the fabric. Measurements include ¼"-wide seam allowances.

1. Fold the black-and-white and multicolored base fabrics as shown and trim so the length is 50".

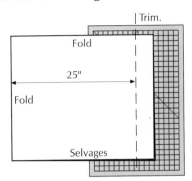

2. Fold the base fabrics as shown to cut the strips, removing the left selvage first.

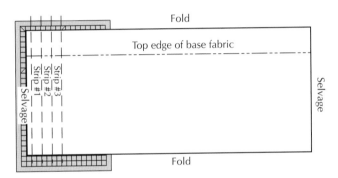

NOTE: Choosing which base fabric to cut first depends on which one you would like to have at the edge of your quilt. Start with the fabric you want at the left edge. Place the strips in sequence as you cut them.

3. From the black-and-white base fabric, cut 21 strips, each 1¾" x 50". Pin each strip in position on your design wall, spacing them 3½" apart to allow room for the multicolored base strips and the filler strips.

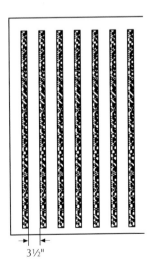

4. From the multicolored floral base fabric, cut 20 strips, each 1¾" x 50". Beginning with the second black-and-white strip, position a multicolored strip on the *left* side of each black-and-white strip, except the first one.

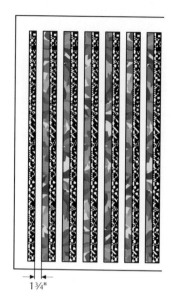

1¾"

You can sew 2 adjacent base-fabric strips together without pinning them first; just be careful not to push or pull them when you feed them under the presser foot. Start sewing at the top edge, leaving a long thread tail as a reminder of where you started. At the end of the seam, clip the thread tail short. Press the seam allowances toward the darker base fabric.

Pin the sewn strips back in place on your design wall, leaving 1¾" between them for the filler strips. Repeat with the remaining pairs of base strips. To avoid mixing them up, do not work on more than 1 pair at a time.

Long thread tails
at top of strips

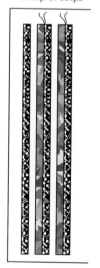

5. From selected fabrics, cut 60 filler strips, each 1¾" x 17", from the lengthwise grain.

6. Overlap the strips on the design wall by ¼" to ⅜" on either side of the color blocks to make it easier to critique the design. Also, look at your design from a distance. Keep in mind that certain visual illusions take time to emerge; give yourself time to adjust.

ASSEMBLING THE QUILT TOP

Working from left to right (or vice versa) and on 1 block unit at a time, sew the quilt top together. A block unit consists of 3 vertical strips: 1 multicolored, 1 black-and-white, and 3 filler strips sewn into 1 strip unit.

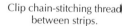

Block Unit

1. Chain-piece each set of 3 filler strips together to make 50"-long strip units. Finger-press the seam allowances toward the darker fabric. The seam allowance with the long thread tail is the one closest to the top of the color-block strip unit.

Clip chain-stitching thread between strips.

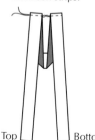

Top   Bottom

2. Pin the color-block strip unit to the adjacent pair of base strips; stitch from top to bottom. Press the seam allowances toward the darker fabric. It is OK to press vertical seam allowances in opposite directions.

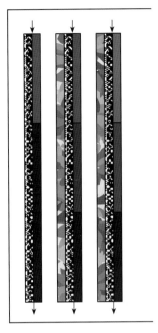

Stitch from top
to bottom.

3. Mark the horizontal seam lines of the color-block strip unit on the outer edge of the adjacent multicolored base strip.

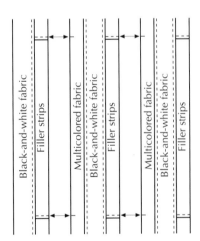

4. Pin the blocks together, starting at the top edge. Align the marks on the multicolored strips with the horizontal seam lines. The horizontal seam lines and top and bottom edges of the color strips should line up across the surface of the quilt top. Sew, stitching from bottom to top. Press the seam allowances toward the darker fabric.

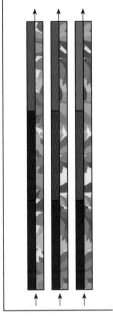

Stitch from
bottom to top.

5. Sew the blocks into larger panels, then join the panels to make the quilt top.

FINISHING

1. Use a long ruler to straighten the bottom edges of the quilt top. Mark a horizontal line even with the shortest strips. Staystitch ⅛" from the line and cut on the line.

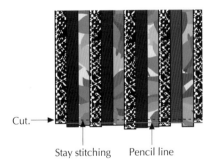

Cut.

Stay stitching   Pencil line

2. Layer the top with batting and backing.
3. Pin-baste with 1" safety pins for machine quilting. Space pins 3" to 5" apart.
4. Quilt as desired, either in-the-ditch or with topstitching as well.
5. Bind the edges of the quilt and add top and bottom sleeves. Inserting a wooden slat into the bottom sleeve to add weight helps the quilt hang straight.
6. Label your quilt.

AMISH CENTER DIAMOND

By Liza Prior Lucy

Meet the Teacher

*L*iza Prior Lucy has always been drawn to the repetition of shape and the riot of colors in scrap quilts, and to the bold simplicity and unconventional color combinations in Amish quilts. In her 20s, Liza was a needlepoint designer, basing many of her canvasses on quilt patterns. When Liza entered her 30s, she turned to knitting and again used quilt designs for inspiration. During that time, she became friends with Kaffe Fassett. Liza learned from him that maverick colors added to a mix of similar tones yields exciting results. It was with this background that Liza hit her 40s running straight into quilting.

Liza prefers simple patterns. When tired and no longer capable of stitching, Liza leafs through her books to absorb ideas. Often, she is drawn to the Amish Center Diamond and Square pattern. One color scheme in particular beckoned her: acid green, cobalt blue, and tomato red. Liza didn't think she could ever be happy working with three solid colors, then eureka! She combined the color concepts of Kaffe Fassett, the piecing techniques of Deirdre Amsden, and the Amish "sparkle" ideas of Roberta Horton.

Liza's student Sharleen Fredericks stayed up all night to finish her quilt. Sharleen's quilt is more subtle than Liza's, and she arranged the fabrics so they would shade from light to dark.

Liza feels that any real "Class Act" is not when students copy the teacher's original, but when the teachers original is merely a launching pad for individual creativity.

TEACHER'S QUILT:
Center Diamond
by Liza Prior Lucy,
1995, Bucks County,
Pennsylvania, 36" x 36".

STUDENT'S QUILT:
Center Diamond
by Sharleen Fredericks,
1995, Bucks County,
Pennsylvania, 36" x 36".

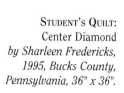

Finished Quilt Size: 36" x 36"

NOTE: You can make the squares any size you wish. Many of Liza's students used leftovers from Colourwash projects. Since those squares were 2" x 2" and finished 1½" x 1½", their projects were smaller than "Center Diamond."

Materials: *44"-wide fabric*

Find a picture of an Amish Center Diamond quilt with a color combination that appeals to you. Let it be your guide to selecting the colors for your quilt.

When selecting fabrics within a color family, choose colors that are close in tone and intensity, but also throw in some related but clashing or maverick colors. For example, if tomato red is one of your colors, use mostly tomato reds, but include magenta, deep orange, and even an occasional yellow-orange.

½ yd. total assorted fabrics for center diamond
½ yd. total assorted fabrics for diamond background
¼ yd. total assorted fabrics for inner borders
¾ yd. total assorted fabrics for outer borders
¼ yd. total assorted fabrics for outer-border corners
1¼ yds. for backing
⅜ yd. for binding
40" x 40" piece of batting

Cutting

Cut squares and triangles using your rotary cutter and ruler. If you prefer to use templates, make plastic or cardboard templates of the square and triangle on the pullout pattern. Trace around the shapes and cut out.

Section	Squares		Triangles
	2½" x 2½"	2⅞" x 2⅞"	
Center Diamond	40	10	20 ◸
Diamond Background	40	10	20 ◿
Inner-Border Sides	40	—	—
Inner-Border Corners	4	—	—
Outer-Border Sides	144	—	—
Outer-Border Corners	36	—	—

NOTE: Cut a few extra squares and triangles from each color so you have pieces to play with when creating your design.

Assembling the Quilt Top & Finishing

1. Arrange the squares and triangles on a design wall. Play with the pieces, rearranging them as necessary until you are pleased with the arrangement.
2. Sew the triangles together and return them to the wall.
3. For ease in construction, sew the squares together in 4 quadrants, 9 x 9 squares each. Beginning in the upper left corner, sew 9 squares together for the first row, then sew 9 squares together for the second row. Repeat for the remaining 7 rows. Press the seams in opposite directions from row to row. When you have completed 9 rows, sew the rows together to form the upper left quadrant.

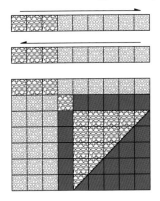

4. Repeat step 3 for the remaining quadrants. Join the 4 quadrants to complete the quilt top.

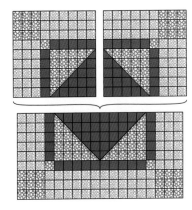

5. Layer the quilt top with batting and backing; baste.
6. Quilt as desired. Liza quilted straight lines in diagonal rows.
7. Bind the edges and label your quilt.

LINDY'S QUILT

By Elaine S. Skierka

Elaine & Kate

TEACHER'S QUILT: Lindy's Quilt *by Elaine S. Skierka, 1993, West Sacramento, California, 41" x 50".*

Meet the Teacher

*E*laine has been quilting seriously since 1986, after learning that quick-piecing methods replaced some of the more time-consuming aspects of individual piecing. Elaine is a busy wife, mother, and grandmother who loves to teach quilting. Sharing her knowledge and love of quilting with students of all levels is a delight, but beginner's are her favorites.

"Lindy's Quilt" started as a Christmas gift for a friend, who just happens to own Quilters' Corner in Sacramento. Elaine drew Lindy's name for the annual gift exchange and wondered, "What do you make for someone who was your quilting teacher?"

Elaine decided to make a Christmas wall hanging, incorporating the Bear Paw block from the store's logo and her favorite star block, the Sawtooth Star, for the border. The Nine Patch blocks are perfect corners for the alternating red and white outer border.

The quilt was a labor of love that turned into a great project. Elaine has plans to make another for a baby quilt. To make a different size, adjust the size of the blocks or make a different number of blocks.

Kate Mackensen was in the first beginning quilting class Elaine taught in 1993. Since then, Kate has become a good friend and teaching assistant. Only to a quilting buddy could Elaine say, "I need you to finish this quilt so we can put it in a book." Not only was it done in time, it also won a second-place ribbon in the local quilt show!

STUDENT'S QUILT:
Pause for the Stars
*by Kate Mackensen, 1995,
Sacramento, California,
40" x 48".*

Finished Quilt Size: 41" x 50"

MATERIALS: *44"-wide fabric*

2 yds. beige print for blocks and inner and outer borders
⅓ yd. red solid for Bear Paw blocks
½ yd. green solid for Sawtooth Star blocks
1¼ yds. red plaid for setting triangles and outer borders
⅜ yd. green print for folded inner borders
1½ yds. for backing
½ yd. for binding
45" x 55" piece of batting

CUTTING

Cut all strips across the fabric width (crosswise grain).

From the beige print, cut:

1 strip, 1½" x 42"; crosscut into 24 squares, each 1½" x 1½", for Bear Paw piece A
3 strips, each 1⅞" x 42"; crosscut into 48 squares, each 1⅞" x 1⅞"; for Bear Paw piece B
2 strips, each 1½" x 42"; crosscut into 24 rectangles, each 1½" x 3½", for Bear Paw piece C
2 strips, each 1½" x 42", for Bear Paw four-patch units
2 squares, each 7½" x 7½", for quilt center
11 strips, each 2" x 42"; crosscut into 224 squares, each 2" x 2", for Sawtooth Star piece E
1 strip, 2" x 42"; crosscut into 2 strips, each 2" x 8", and 1 strip, 2" x 16", for Nine Patch blocks
8 strips, each 2" x 42", for outer border

From the red solid, cut:

3 strips, each 1⅞" x 42"; crosscut into 48 squares, each 1⅞" x 1⅞", for Bear Paw piece B
2 strips, each 1½" x 42", for Bear Paw four-patch units
6 squares, each 1½" x 1½", for Bear Paw piece D

From the green solid, cut:

7 strips, each 1¼" x 42"; crosscut into 224 squares, each 1¼" x 1¼", for Sawtooth Star piece F
2 strips, each 2" x 42"; crosscut into 28 squares, each 2" x 2", for Sawtooth Star piece G

From the green print, cut:

8 strips, each 1" x 42", for folded inner borders

From the red plaid, cut:

2 squares, each 14" x 14"; cut twice diagonally to yield 8 quarter-square triangles for side triangles (You will use 6.)
2 squares, each 9" x 9"; cut once diagonally to yield 4 half-square triangles for corner triangles
1 strip, 2" x 42"; crosscut into 2 strips, each 2" x 16", and strip, 2" x 8", for Nine Patch blocks
4 strips, each 2" x 42", for outer border

BEAR PAW BLOCKS

Finished Block Size: 7" x 7"

1. Draw a diagonal line on the wrong side of the 1⅞" beige squares. Place a marked square on top of a 1⅞" red solid square, right sides together. Stitch ¼" from both sides of the drawn line.

2. Cut on the drawn line. Press the seams toward the red triangle and trim the dog-ear corners. Each pair of squares yields 2 half-square triangle units. Make a total of 96 half-square triangle units.

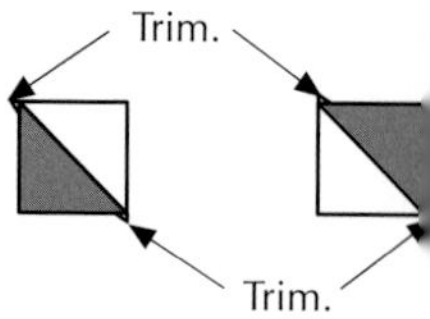

3. Sew a 1½"-wide beige strip to a 1½"-wide red solid strip to make a strip unit. Press the seam toward the red strip. Make 2 strip units. Cut a total of 48 segments, each 1½" wide, from the strip units. Sew 2 segments together as shown to make a four-patch unit. Make a total of 24 four-patch units.

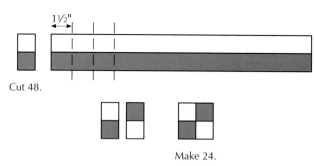

Cut 48.

Make 24.

4. Join 4 four-patch units, 16 half-square triangle units (piece B), 4 piece A, 4 piece C, and 1 piece D as shown to make a Bear Paw block. Make a total of 6 blocks.

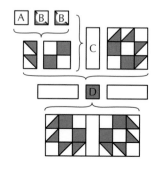
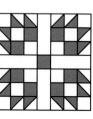

Make 6.

Sawtooth Star Blocks

Finished Block Size: 4½" x 4½"

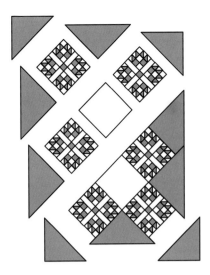

1. Draw a diagonal line on the wrong side of each 1¼" green solid square. Place a marked green square on the bottom right corner of a 2" beige square. Sew on the line, trim the seam to ¼", and press the seam toward the green triangle. To make a star-point unit, repeat with a second green square on the bottom left corner of the beige square. Make a total of 112 star-point units.

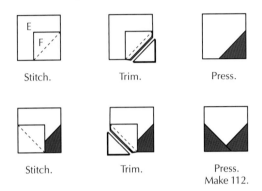

Stitch.   Trim.   Press.

Stitch.   Trim.   Press.
Make 112.

2. Join 4 star-point units, 4 piece E, and 1 piece G as shown to make a Sawtooth Star block. Make a total of 28 blocks.

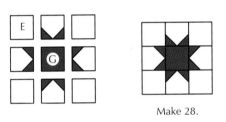

Make 28.

Assembling the Quilt Top

1. Arrange the Bear Paw blocks, 7½" beige print squares, and side and corner triangles as shown above right. The side and corner triangles are oversized so the blocks appear to float on the red plaid background. The triangles will be trimmed in the next step.

   Sew the blocks and side triangles together in diagonal rows. Press the seams in opposite directions from row to row. Join the rows, making sure to match the seams between the blocks. Add the corner triangles last.

2. Trim the quilt top to 23" x 32" so the pieced Sawtooth Star borders will fit. Measure the width and length of the quilt through the center; note the measurements. Subtract the required measurements from the actual measurements you noted. Divide the difference of each measurement by 2; this is the amount to trim from each edge. Trim equal amounts from opposite sides, otherwise the Bear Paw Blocks will not be centered. Use a long ruler and rotary cutter to trim the edges.

NOTE: If your Sawtooth Star blocks did not finish to 4½", wait until you have assembled the Sawtooth Star border strips before measuring and trimming the edges of your quilt top. For the sides, measure the length of 7 Sawtooth Star blocks sewn together. For the top and bottom, measure the length of 5 Sawtooth Star blocks sewn together. Subtract these measurements from the actual measurements of your quilt top, divide by 2, and trim the appropriate amounts from each edge. Remember, trim equal amounts from opposite sides.

Adding the Borders

1. Fold the 1" green print strips in half lengthwise; press. Trim 2 folded strips to match the length of the quilt (32"), and 2 strips to match the width (23"). Aligning the raw edges, baste the strips to the sides first, then to the top and bottom edges of the quilt top.
2. Join the Sawtooth Star blocks into 4 rows of 7 stars each.
3. Sew the Sawtooth Star borders to the sides first, then to the top and bottom edges. Press the seams toward the pieced borders. The folded strips should lay toward the quilt center.

Folded borders
basted in place

4. Fold the remaining 1" green print strips in half length-wise; press. Measure the width and length of the quilt through the center, including the borders just added. Note the measurements (they should be 32" x 42"). Trim the folded strips to match. Aligning the raw edges, baste the strips to the sides first, then to the top and bottom edges of the quilt top.
5. Sew a 2" x 8" beige strip to each side of a 2" x 8" red plaid strip to make a strip unit. Cut 4 segments, each 2" wide, from the strip unit. Sew a 2" x 16" red plaid strip to each side of a 2" x 16" beige strip to make a second strip unit. Cut 8 segments, each 2" wide, from this strip unit.

Cut 4.

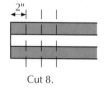

Cut 8.

6. Join the segments as shown to make 4 Nine Patch blocks.

Make 4.

7. Join the 2" x 42" beige strips and 2" x 42" red plaid strips as shown to make 4 border strips.

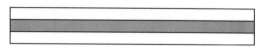

Make 4.

8. Trim the pieced border strips to the measurements noted in step 4. Sew the longest border strips to the sides. Add a Nine Patch block to each end of the remaining border strips, and sew these to the top and bottom edges.

Folded bord
basted in pl

Finishing

1. Layer quilt top with batting and backing; baste.
2. Quilt as desired.
3. Bind the edges and label your quilt.